Advance Pr
Choosing C

D0563171

"This book is simple and practical – that is Kim's genius I think – to make life-changing principles simple enough for anyone to understand and practical enough for everyone to use. A definite must read for anyone seeking lasting change in their life!"

~Matt Townsend, Ph.D.,
Relationship Coach & Radio Show Host

"We cannot always choose what happens, but we can choose how to respond. This book lays out a clear and simple approach to eliminating fear and promoting trust. By reading and doing the activities presented, you will improve your relationships and be more successful in your life."

~Russell C. Gaede, PsyD,
Speaker, Author, Therapist

"Kim Giles gives you the tools and information to address your self-defeating thoughts and habits to actually make a change. And her training, knowledge, insights and personal experiences come through in her book, *Choosing Clarity*. In the book she asks you to truly look at yourself and to look at who you think you are and who you really can be. The chapters in the book will challenge your thinking and your motivations. Then fill you with self-awareness and a new freedom.

"In *Choosing Clarity* Kim doesn't just preach principles – she tells you how to apply them. She teaches how to overcome fear and disappointment, how to love, how to find yourself, how to trust and how to come out stronger and happier."

~Don Hudson,
News Anchor and Reporter, KTVX - TV

"Choosing love over fear works every time. You can't go wrong when you focus on other people instead of yourself."

~Chad Hymas,
CPAE, Hall of Fame Speaker

"Kim Giles's book *Choosing Clarity: The Path to Fearlessness* is not just a light bulb in support of the power of love and fear; it's a big, bright lighthouse that serves as a beacon of hope for those of us who need a practical, day-to-day, lifetime approach for addressing our fears and letting love rule. Read this book and apply the principles to your personal life, romantic relationships and your business life – the results will amaze you. Just apply it!"

~Winn Claybaugh, Dean & Cofounder of Paul Mitchell Schools,
Speaker and Author of *BE NICE (OR ELSE!)*

"You must believe me when I say I have experienced tragedy beyond imagination. This material has given me more peace than I have had in years. I now see that I have not passed or failed the test of life, but instead completed some extremely difficult classes. This system has helped me live a life of more happiness than I have had in almost two decades. Learning to look at life through trust and love will bring you peace!"

~Jennifer Lyle,
Vice President, Sailing The Blues, Inc.

"The principles this book is built on are what make it so effective. They are true principles. Because of that, they will help anyone who wants to improve their relationships and heal what's hurting them. The formulas and tools give life to these principles. Use them – This program works."

~Phyllis Allem

"The Claritypoint principles have changed the way I view myself and the world around me. The formulas and tools really work if you apply them. Your "victim" thinking habits will change and you will find you can take charge of your life. Even past failures, when the tools are used, become stepping stones for fulfillment and achievement. I highly recommend *Choosing Clarity* for anyone with an honest desire to increase self-esteem and heal your relationships."

~Joani Evans,
Business Owner

"I use the formulas and principles in *Choosing Clarity* every day. I use them at work and even when handling situations with my teenager. I have learned how to overcome my fears, find happiness within myself, thanks to the Clarity Formula. I am a new and improved me."

~Hollie Firth,
Retail Store Manager

"I have nothing but positive things to say about this information! The principles Kim teaches are basic and universal, but her formulas, tools and worksheets clarify how those principles relate to you personally and how you can implement them in your own life. Once implemented, they are honestly life-changing. They have transformed me, my marriage and the way I look at life. I'm so grateful."

~Brianna McFarland,
Wife & Mother

"I can't say "Thank You" enough! The tools and formulas in this book are life savers. I still use them and reference them every day. I have two young boys who are currently learning the Clarity points for Confident Kids too. I couldn't be happier – your principles, formulas and tools have taught me how to live life to the fullest. Thank you, Coach Kim."

~Sheri H.,
Business Owner

"*Choosing Clarity* empowered me to approach current challenges in a healthier, more productive way. Thanks for blessing my life. I can't wait for others to read it."

~Brad Barton, CSP, Inspirational Keynote Speaker

"These principles are making my life so much better, they are filled with wonderful information, even for a sixty-nine year old woman – you can teach an old dog new tricks. The Universal truths that Kim teaches in a step by step format, are a profound and joyous way to see life, filled with awe and freedom from fear, pain and anguish. I can now feel my value and understand that what we call bad behavior is really a cry for real acceptance. My great thanks and gratitude for Kimberly Giles."

~Dawne Hole

"Kim's universally true principles of human worth and courage empower each of us to gain safe ground despite the perils we may face. These principles, combined with her powerful tools to utilize them in daily living, create a one-two punch that, with practice, can lift any person, man or woman, from fear to safety. **I cannot recommend these principles and tools highly enough.** They incorporate the best of humanity and take those who are willing to make the journey into a place where faith, courage and hope take center stage over their opposite and crippling counterfeits, despair, fear and hopelessness. Please take a chance to change yourself, read this book... and then go and change the world!"

~Mark Richards,
Business Owner

"I've always been a nice, happy person on the outside, but inside I was confused, broken and felt unloved. I allowed others' negative actions to cause me tremendous pain. I wasn't true to myself and when I was, I felt guilty. This program and especially *The Clarity Formula*, has helped me realize that there are different ways to think and react in life that can bring peace. The principles seem obvious and simple, but they change lives. Now, I have more confidence and trust than I have ever had before. I now have the tools to help me see myself, others and life in a true and clear way."

~Ann Whimpy, Wife and Mother

"Kim has taken foundational principles that apply to every aspect of a person's life and organized them in a way that allows for easy understanding and application. Whether in our homes, our neighborhood, our community, our church, or in the work place, these principles, when understood and applied, result in being able to more fully understand ourselves, others, and God. The formulas make it possible for us to see where change is needed, and at the same time, guide us through the change process."

~Kirk Godfrey, Educator, Trainer and Life Coach

"As Kim's Mom I have watched her help people with every kind of problem imaginable and I've seen this program work for all of them. I am so proud of her and the difference she is making in the lives of so many. Read this book and try what she teaches for yourself, this book might be all you need."

~Pam McCullough

"This book is spot-on. Fear can freeze us from the life we are meant to live. Kim Giles's insightful recipe will help everyone compile the right ingredients to live a life without fear, full of clarity and hope."

~Marti Skold, Anchor, News 14 Carolina

Choosing Clarity

THE PATH TO FEARLESSNESS

by Kimberly Giles

THOMAS NOBLE BOOKS

Copyright © 2014 by Kimberly Giles

All rights reserved. No part of this book may be used or reproduced in any manner whatsoever without written permission from the author, except by a reviewer who may quote brief passages for review purposes.

For more information about this book or the author, visit:

www.ClarityPointCoaching.com

Thomas Noble Books
427 N Tatnall Street #90946
Wilmington, DE 19801-2230
636-922-2634

Library of Congress Control Number: 2013957119

ISBN 978-0-9892357-7-8

Printed in the United States of America

First Printing 2014

Editing by Gwen Hoffnagle

Cover Design by Cyanotype.ca

This book is dedicated to
my amazing father who taught me
to be fearless and
my wonderful mother who
taught me love.

Table of Contents

Disclaimer

Throughout this book there are stories about Kim's coaching clients. The names and situations have been drastically changed to protect their privacy, but their results are real.

About the Author

Kimberly Giles is a sought-after executive coach, author, and speaker. She is the president and founder of Claritypoint Life Coaching and a popular TV and radio personality. She was named one of the top twenty Advice Gurus in the Country by Good Morning America in 2010 because of her unique perspective on and ideas about life. Since then hundreds of her articles have been published in newspapers and magazines.

Kimberly's unique perspective was influenced by the work of Viktor Frankl, the author of *Man's Search for Meaning* and the founder of logotherapy. His story of survival in concentration camps during World War II greatly impacted Kimberly as she struggled through difficult challenges and periods of suffering in her own life. Her journey hasn't been an easy one. She has battled chronic illness and a whole spectrum of problems and trials. But it was these challenges that facilitated her discovering the life-changing formulas you are about to learn. She has taken the principles Dr. Frankl taught and used them to develop a simple system for healthy thinking and happy living. She was also influenced by the Course in Miracles, which helped her see that overcoming fear is the key to happiness and success.

Kimberly was also greatly influenced by the work of Dr. Robert Hartman, the father of axiology. There is a version of the Hartman Value Profile Assessment available at her website for those who want to understand how their fears affect their subconscious thinking. You can take it for free at http://www.claritypointcoaching.com.

Claritypoint Coaching provides executive life coaching and corporate training to individuals and organizations interested in eliminating fear. The company also offers Coach Certification to those interested in facilitating the Claritypoint program.

Introduction

This book has the power to change your life in a profound and permanent way. It is going to do this by teaching you a simple system for thinking clearly and seeing the world more accurately. *Choosing Clarity* is a life-coaching process through which you have the opportunity to change some of your deeply held beliefs and attitudes about yourself and life.

Changing these attitudes and writing some new personal policies and procedures will release you from fear and help you make better choices, create better relationships, and experience more peace. Eliminating fear will also do wonders for your career, because fear is hampering your creativity, innovation, and drive. It is holding you back from being the real, best you.

I know this system for gaining Clarity and eliminating fear will work for you because it worked for me. It has completely changed my life and business for the better. It has also worked for thousands of people and companies who have used it around the world. Other coaches are now using this process with their clients and experiencing equal success. But you must do more than just read this book for it to work; you must take the time to write the personal policies and procedures it recommends. *If you do this, it will change everything.*

No matter what kind of challenges you are facing, no matter the size or scope of the problems in your life, this book will help you see them from a different perspective, and you will discover, as I have, two fundamental truths about life:

1. Most of your suffering is self-inflicted.
2. Every problem you face is really a fear problem.

Fear causes problems in your life because it fogs or skews the lens through which you see yourself and your world. Obviously, if you can't see yourself, situations, or other people accurately, you won't respond in an appropriate way or make good decisions. You will also suffer (and suffer greatly) because you think suffering is your only choice. *Choosing Clarity* will help you see that you have the power to choose not to suffer.

In *Choosing Clarity* I play the role of your "mental ophthalmologist" (an idea that came from Viktor Frankl) and help you clear away the fog of fear so you can see yourself, other people, and your life more accurately than you have ever seen them before. When this happens, you will finally see why you are choosing suffering and how to choose peace, happiness, and success instead.

Choosing Clarity addresses in particular the fear of failure (the fear of not being good enough), something I believe every person on this planet battles on a daily basis. Eliminating this fear is the greatest gift I could give you because this fear is the biggest thing in your way. Most people spend the majority of their lives (almost every second of every day) battling this fear because they don't know how to escape it. *Choosing Clarity* shows you *exactly* how to escape this fear and create unshakable self-esteem in the process. My hope is that this book will give you all the tools you need to eliminate your fear of failure and stop being afraid that you aren't good enough.

But *Choosing Clarity* not only addresses your conscious fears, it also teaches you how to remove fear from your subconscious mind. This is important because your success and happiness is largely determined by the quality of your subconscious programming. Neuroscience now tells us that 95 percent of your thoughts and choices are actually controlled by your subconscious mind. This means you are running on autopilot (unconscious) most of the time. The reason you might not be creating the life you want is that you are making most of your decisions unconsciously, and most of your subconscious policies (programs and rules) are fear-based and inaccurate. These inaccurate policies are sabotaging your success because they don't want the very things you think you consciously want.

Have you ever felt like you have one foot on the gas and one foot on the brake? Are you getting nowhere, yet you know YOU are the problem? If so, you probably have some subconscious programs that are fighting against you and need to be realigned. The good news is that you can change these programs and therefore change your life, and it's easier than you'd think.

As you begin this process to change your subconscious policies you might find it difficult at first; you might think it feels impossible to change. Don't worry if you feel this way. It only feels impossible because you have been living in fear for a long time and you have become very good at it. *Fear has become your comfort zone.* You might even believe that you can't change and that your subconscious fears are out of your control, but they aren't. You can change them. And in doing so, you can change the way you feel about everything, especially yourself. I will show you exactly how to do this.

You must do more than just read this book, though. I strongly encourage you to use it as a life-coaching process and take the time to create a set of policies and procedures for your life and read them daily. If you do this, you will start feeling better fast. I promise. Writing new official personal policies based in trust and love will change how you feel and give you the Clarity you need to create the results you want. *But the system won't work if you don't do the work.* Please stop and write policies about every topic you come to and reread your personal policies daily.

There is a reason that every successful organization and company has a set of clearly defined policies and procedures outlining their mindset, their intent, their mission, and their conduct. Organizations create and integrate their policies and procedures so their behavior will be consistent, appropriate, and productive across the board. They understand that having clearly defined policies is the foundation of success. Through reading *Choosing Clarity*, you will have the opportunity to write a new set of policies and procedures for your life that will create the same kind of solid foundation for you. Please get a small notebook to use as your official policies and procedures book or you can download a worksheet for this from **www.claritypointcoaching.com**

Your new personal policies and procedures will define how you see and value yourself, God, people, life, relationships, and work. They will outline how you will respond to every situation that shows up in your life. Having these policies and procedures based on your values, clearly defined ahead of time, will make you feel competent, confident, and capable in every situation. They will give you some much needed solid ground to stand on.

Throughout the course of your life you have been creating policies and procedures without knowing you were doing it. Everything you experienced as a child planted rules or policies into your subconscious mind, and you accepted these rules as facts. Most of these policies were adopted as rules before you were even five years old. Since then you have been reacting to situations unconsciously with these ideas guiding your actions.

Let me explain how this happens. Maybe one day before you left the house your mother said, *"Don't go out like that! What will the neighbors think of us?"*

In that moment you might have adopted a policy that said, *"What other people think of me is something to fear."*

You may have spent your entire life afraid of other people and their judgments. *Did this happen to you?* Most of us still battle this subconscious program on a daily basis. Below are some other fear-based subconscious policies you might have adopted as a child. Read through them and circle the ones that resonate with you.

- All men are trouble and can't be trusted.
- Women are all liars and after your money.
- If I don't make enough money, I have no value.
- If I make too much money, I'm greedy.
- People aren't safe. They can't be trusted.
- If other people think badly of me, it is literally the end of the world.
- It's safer not to stick your neck out.
- If a man gets emotional it means he is weak.
- It's better not to try than to risk rejection.
- I'm never going to be good enough no matter how hard I try. So I might as well not try at all.
- I can't help how I feel.
- If this one person doesn't love me, no one will.
- I don't deserve any better than this.
- If I don't have a man in my life, I have no value.
- Shooting high is dangerous and means you're arrogant.
- You shouldn't toot your own horn.

- You shouldn't be proud of yourself, or you're arrogant.
- You should never make other people feel bad, or you're a bad person.

You did not consciously choose to believe these inaccurate ideas. They were planted in your head by feelings and impressions you had. You may even consciously know they aren't accurate, but your subconscious mind still believes them. Now they have become your foggy lens and they are silently directing the course of your life, holding you back at work, and wreaking havoc in your relationships. But don't worry. As I said before, *you can change them.*

Throughout *Choosing Clarity* I will teach you how to use trust and love, the opposites of fear, to eliminate fear from your thinking and experience more Clarity and less suffering in your life. You have the power to override your subconscious programs of fear and choose how you want to feel. You have the power to choose your mindset in every moment, and this choice is a simple one because there are only two options: *a fear perspective or a love perspective.*

I include trust as part of love because you can't experience love (you are not even capable of love) until you trust in something that takes away your fear. Trust and love together are the complete opposites of fear, and once you learn how to live in trust and love (which is not hard to do after reading this book) you will see clearly how to create the life you want.

This simple concept is one of the most important in the book – in every moment you get to decide how you want to feel and experience the situation, and it is a simple choice because there are only two options:

FEAR	TRUST & LOVE
foggy lens	clear lens
inaccurate	accurate
selfish	capable of love
unconsciousness	consciousness
suffering	joy

How do you want to live?

You do not always get to choose the circumstances in your life. You often have to go through things you would rather not do. *But you always get to choose how you will experience those circumstances.* I learned this powerful truth from studying the work of Dr. Frankl, who survived Nazi concentration camps in the worst conditions imaginable and found he had the power to choose his attitude even there.

He understood these two options well. He could choose love, which would create dignity, morality, and peace, or he could choose fear, which would create suffering, hopelessness, and pain. Either way his situation was the same. Dr. Frankl said:

> We who lived in concentration camps can remember the men who walked through the huts comforting others, giving away their last piece of

bread. They may have been few in number, but they offer sufficient proof that everything can be taken from a man but one thing: the last of the human freedoms – to choose one's attitude in any given set of circumstances, to choose one's own way. And there were always choices to make. Every day, every hour, offered the opportunity to make a decision which determined whether you would, or would not, submit to those powers which threatened to rob you of your very self, your inner freedom; which determined whether or not you would become the plaything of circumstance renouncing freedom and dignity.[1]

Every moment of your life you are faced with this same choice. You can either experience the moment in fear and most likely behave in a selfish, immature, and dramatic way, or you can experience it in trust (feeling safe) and behave in a wise, mature, strong, and loving way. The question is *how do you want to live? How do you want to experience the moment?* These two questions are the foundation of this book.

Choosing Clarity will teach you exactly *how* to choose trust and love in every situation. It will tell you exactly how to replace your negative fear-based thoughts and what to replace them with.

This system has already worked for thousands of people around the world who have tried it. It has worked for housewives, business executives, corporations, couples, soccer moms, college students, and inmates. It doesn't matter what specific difficulties you are experiencing – learning to choose *Clarity* (trust and love) in every situation will make your life better.

You will notice, as you go through this book that everything I teach is based on a principle of truth. Most of these principles of truth are already familiar to you, though you might not have seen them put together this way. Once you learn the principles the way I explain them, you will see them everywhere. You will see them in scripture, in self-help books, and playing out in the lives of everyone around you. You will wonder how you didn't see them before.

I call the principles in the book clarity**points** because they are points that bring *Clarity*. As you read *Choosing Clarity* and are introduced to each clarity**point** principle, I urge you to take a minute to listen to what your *inner truth* has to say about it. Don't take my word for anything. Ask your heart if these principles feel like truth to you. Listen to your gut feelings and base your new policies and procedures on your personal beliefs.

I will challenge you to reexamine some of your beliefs and check them for accuracy, though. You must make sure you aren't experiencing your beliefs in a fear-based way. I urge you to be open to looking at all your beliefs from a love perspective, but remember this process is not about changing what you believe. It is about making sure that you are experiencing what you believe accurately (in trust and love) and that your subconscious policies are in line with truth.

I use the terms below throughout this book. Take a minute to be sure you understand them as I define them.

Policy: a rule, program, or intent of conduct relative to a specific situation or behavior

Procedure: a process or course of action based on policy that assures the policy is carried out

Clarity: the state of being clear as to perception or understanding; the ability to see things accurately

Trust: reliance on the integrity, strength, ability, and surety of something or someone

Love: care, value, honor, respect, and validation of yourself and others

If you will not just read this book, but take the time to carefully craft a new set of personal policies and procedures based in *Clarity*, and read through your policies at least once every day, you won't believe how drastically your life will change. Are you ready to start the process? Turn the page and let's get started!

I – Fear Is the Problem

I wrote earlier that every problem you are currently facing is a fear problem. Let me explain how that works by sharing a story from one of my life-coaching clients.

> Carol was having problems getting along with her business partner. She hoped some coaching would help her get rid of the anger she was feeling before it destroyed their business. My first question for her was "What are you afraid of when you are around your partner?" "Nothing," she replied. "I just don't like him and can't deal with his negative attitude."
>
> I tried again. "What does his negativity make you afraid of?" Carol had to think about this for a minute. Then she started to see that her partner's negative attitude triggered her fear of failure (her fear of not being good enough). She was afraid that her partner's unhappiness was her fault; that at some level her own faults were causing the problem. These fears were creating anger, resentment, and a feeling of impending doom at work. Carol's problem was a fear problem. Her fear of not being good enough was being projected onto her partner. Fear was skewing her perspective of this situation.

The goal of *Choosing Clarity* is very simple; it is to show you how to clear away the fear that has been skewing your vision so you can see your life more accurately. The first step in this process is to become conscious of your subconscious fears (especially the two core fears) that cause most of your problems.

Take a minute to think about the last time you made a mistake or said something stupid. Have you ever tripped in public or been embarrassed? Did your face turn red? Do you remember how that experience felt? Do you know why these experiences are so painful?

It's because they trigger what is already your deepest, darkest core fear – *the fear that you might not be good enough.* Think about those words for a minute. Can you recognize this is fear in you? Do you often feel inadequate or deficient in some way? Do you sometimes feel not as good as other people? Are you afraid you're failing in some aspect of your life? Are you ever afraid you're just not good enough?

There are just so many levels on which you can fail or come up short. You can be not smart enough, pretty enough, successful enough, brave enough, cool enough, or athletic enough. You can fail as a parent, a spouse, a friend, a student, or in business. No matter how hard you try in one area you are probably falling short in another. You just can't *be enough* to make this fear go away.

I believe this fear was planted in your subconscious mind when you were just a small child. No matter what kind of kid you were (or how fantastic your parents were), you heard things like *Don't do that! Can't you just sit still? Be quiet. Be good. Calm down.* Or *Speak up.* The message was delivered loud and clear, in a hundred different ways – *you need to be different than you are. Who you are isn't good enough.*

As you grew, this fear may have developed into a fear of failure, a fear of looking bad, and a fear of judgment. When you became an adult, it became a fear of being rejected or abandoned or unworthy of love. Every time you experienced disappointment, hurt, or shame, this fear got bigger and covered up more of your love, pushing the real you deeper and deeper down to protect you.

No matter how the fear of failure shows up for you today, *this deepest, darkest fear is definitely causing problems in your life and driving unproductive or destructive behavior.* In some people this fear causes social anxiety, insecurity, or shyness. In others it makes them show off or try too hard to get noticed. It could make you overly defensive or protective at times. It could hold you back from taking risks, learning new things, and making decisions. (This fear is the reason it took me six years to finish this book. I just never thought it was good enough.)

Think about what this fear has cost you. How has it stopped you from living fully? Is it taking the joy from your journey because you are always worried about what other people think of you? Does it prevent you from reaching out or connecting with people? Does it make you scared to do things you really want to do?

However it affects you, it isn't positive.

The other core fear that also affects you on a daily basis is *the fear of loss, or the fear that your life isn't going to be good enough.* The fear of loss includes the loss of security, control, money, reputation, loved ones, respect, opportunities, and validation from others. Take a minute to think about how often you experience a fear of being taken from, walked on, or not having your fair share of what you need or deserve.

- How often do you feel mistreated or insulted by other people?
- Do you feel the need to control people or situations to feel safe?
- Are you scared about losing the people in your life?
- Are you scared of not having enough money?
- How do you treat others when this fear gets triggered?

This fear can encourage a lot of controlling, manipulative behavior. It can make you too easily offended, emotional, or reactive. This fear can cause issues in every area of your life.

It is very important that you understand these two core fears *(the fear of failure and the fear of loss)* and how they show up in your life, because they are responsible for a large majority of your subconscious thinking, and therefore a lot of your problems. I believe these two fears together are responsible for about 80 percent of all human behavior. I realize that is a bold statement, but I honestly believe it to be true. Most of the choices you make are driven by the need to quiet these two fears.

Even many of the good things you do are driven by the need to quiet these fears. You might feel motivated to sacrifice and do too much for other people because you want the validation you receive for doing it. You might do things for people so they will feel obligated to like and approve of you. This kind of service is fear motivated and has nothing to do with love.

Throughout this book I refer to the fear of failure and the fear of loss as *your two core fears.* You might want to explore which of the two is a bigger issue for you. Think about what you are most afraid of. Are you more afraid of failing, being rejected, or looking bad? Or are you more afraid of being taken from, losing things, or missing out on something?

If you want to find out exactly how these two core fears drive your subconscious thinking, visit my website and take the free Personal Fear Assessment (www.claritypointcoaching.com). This amazing test will show you exactly where fear is causing problems in your life. Once you become aware of what is happening in your head, you will have the power to change it.

The following are some characteristics of fear-based thinking that will help you see why fear is behind your problems:

1. **Fear keeps you focused on you.** When you experience a fear of failure or loss, you are being

selfish and focused on getting the love, attention, fair treatment, or validation you think you need. You cannot show up for other people when you are in this state. You are not even capable of love. If you spend your day here, you are choosing to be a getter, not a giver, and you will probably miss the needs of other people completely.

2. **Fear encourages you to play small or shoot low.** Fear tells you it's safer to keep the bar low and stay out of the limelight. It encourages you to be less than you are capable of being. This is where fear causes big problems in business, as it can kill innovation, risk taking, and even creativity.

3. **Fear makes you needy.** Fear creates a feeling of lack and scarcity. It makes you jealous of others. When you show up in fear, other people subconsciously feel your neediness and see you as a threat. And you are a threat because you are not capable of focusing on them. If you are a salesperson, this is where fear causes problems in sales because it makes people see you as a threat.

4. **Fear makes you take things personally that aren't personal.** Fear tells you that people who are whispering and then look your way are talking about you. Fear makes you think that everything anyone does or says is a reflection on your value. You literally think that everything that happens is about

you and means you aren't good enough. (*Think about this one.*)

5. **Fear makes you think your value must be earned.** Fear says you need to get validation or recognition from other people in order to feel that you have value. It says you have to earn lots of money or look perfect to be good enough.

6. **Fear is the critic in your head that says you have to be perfect**. It is the voice in your head that judges everything you do and everything other people do. It says if you aren't perfect, you aren't good enough. Since perfect isn't possible, fear always tells you that you aren't good enough.

7. **Fear creates a win/lose mentality.** It makes you think other people have to lose for you to win. It encourages you to compete and compare yourself with others. It says you have to be better than other people to have value.

8. **Fear makes you see other people as different from you.** That means you will see them as either better than you or worse than you. Fear sees everyone you don't like or don't understand as the bad guys so you can feel like the good guy. It spends a lot of time casting other people as the bad guys.

9. **Fear is the root of almost every negative emotion.** Fear is behind anger, jealousy, guilt, suspicion,

rejection, hurt, and pessimism. It is the cause of depression, discouragement, and frustration. It is a place of ego, pride, defensiveness, anxiety, concern, protecting, getting, gaining, and proving your value. It is behind judgment, criticism, conflict, and every other negative state you can experience. *(Can you see why it's a problem?)*

10. **Nothing fear says or encourages is real.** F.E.A.R. is False Evidence Appearing Real. If you step back and clean off your lens, you will see that nothing fear says is accurate.

11. **Fear covers up who you really are.** Fear makes you forget love and hide who you really are deep inside. It literally prevents you from being YOU.

It is important that you understand how fear affects you and how it drives human behavior so you can start to see situations and people accurately and respond more appropriately. When someone is behaving badly, attacking you, or being defensive, critical, or judgmental, it is not really about you. *Fear is the real reason people behave badly.* Their fears make them selfish, defensive, mean, and grouchy. When someone is behaving badly, step back and ask yourself, "What is this person afraid of? What fear inside me is driving my reaction to their attack? What am I afraid of?"

When you can accurately see the fear behind their behavior, and yours, you will see the situation for what it really is. You will also see that what is needed is compassion and understanding, not defensiveness and attack.

clarity**point**: **Fear drives over 80 percent of all human behavior.** There are two core fears that most people experience to some degree on a daily basis. They are:

1) **The fear of not being good enough** (the fear of failure)

2) **The fear that life won't be good enough.** (the fear of loss)

Carol's Story continued:

The only way to change the situation at Carol's office was to get her out of fear and into Clarity. When Carol could accurately see her partner's behavior for what it was – her partner's negative reaction to the two core fears in himself – she could clearly see the problem wasn't about her. This is an important principle of truth.

clarity**point**: **Most bad behavior is about that person's core fears about themselves; it is rarely about you.**

Carol's partner was scared of failure and loss, and these fears were making him miserable and creating all kinds of bad behavior, much of which was directed at her. Since Carol had no control over her partner's attitude, she decided to focus on fixing her own. I took Carol through the exact process I'm about to take you through in this book, and she created a new set of fearless policies and procedures for her life. Now she is no longer bothered by other people's bad moods because she understands they are not about her. They are all about fear.

Now it's your turn to do the same and start seeing your life more accurately. The first step in this process involves looking at your spiritual and/or religious beliefs. You must do this because your spiritual beliefs (or your philosophies about life) deeply affect the way you see the world and value yourself. Most business-appropriate books avoid these topics, but I believe it would do you a disservice to leave them out.

Your subconscious thinking is greatly impacted by your life philosophy or spiritual beliefs. They determine how fear affects you and give purpose and meaning to everything you experience. They also affect the way you value yourself and judge other people. Choosing Clarity gives you the chance to look at your beliefs from a unique perspective, though, and make sure you are experiencing them from a place of love, not fear. This will give you a solid foundation on which to build all your other policies.

Throughout this book I share some of my personal policies, which reflect my personal spiritual beliefs. Please do not be offended by this. I share these only as examples of what trust-and-love-based policies might look like. You should base your personal policies on your own beliefs.

After you have clearly defined who you are and the purpose of your life, we will create policies around your business, relationships, communication, and self-esteem.

2 – What You Believe

More than anything else, I want you to feel better about yourself and your life. I believe if you can understand *how you think* in a more accurate way, you will gain Clarity about your current situation and more peace. But in order to gain Clarity and live your life from a fearless perspective, you must first examine your core beliefs about *who you are* and *why you are here.* This is the first step to changing what's not working in your life.

What you believe about the purpose of your life and who you are greatly affects the way you feel about everything else in your life. I believe that a life philosophy, a religion, or a set of spiritual beliefs can play an important, even critical role in your psychological stability and emotional strength. We, as human beings, seem to do better when we have some kind of context or framework that provides purpose and meaning in our lives. In the book *A Will to Meaning*, Viktor Frankl said that religion makes an "inestimable contribution to mental health. After all, religion provides man with a spiritual anchor, with a feeling of security such as he can find no-where else." Even if you are not interested in organized religion, you still benefit from having a life philosophy or set of beliefs that give meaning and purpose to your experiences and provide that anchor.

For most people this life philosophy includes belief in a higher power of some kind *(though it doesn't matter in what form or by what name you call it).* I personally believe there is a higher power in the universe, and this belief forms the foundation of my personal policies. You can agree with me or you can see this higher power as more of a life force at work in the universe. The specifics don't matter. What is important is that you believe in something that provides context to your life and meaning to your experiences.

I'm going to assume that you do believe in a higher power or energy force in the universe, and throughout the book I will refer to that force as God. You can replace that word, though, with whatever feels right to you.

I also believe there is a force in the universe that opposes God. Almost every religion or life philosophy on the planet defines these *two* forces, though again they call them different names and see them in different forms. I prefer to see these forces as *a fear force* and *a love force.* I believe these two forces provide you with the opportunity to choose, in every moment, how you want to experience your life.

You can experience each situation from fear or you can experience it from love. With only two options, this is really simple. You can see yourself from fear (feeling you are never good enough) or love (feeling you are always good enough). You can experience your religion from fear (where you could be damned) or love (where you are forgiven). You can experience your job from fear (proving your value) or love (serving others). You have these same two options in every situation.

....

claritypoint: **There are two forces in the universe: fear and love.** Trust is part of love because it makes you feel safe, and it is only in this state that you are capable of love.

....

I explain these two forces in great detail throughout *Choosing Clarity*, but for now understand that love is the positive force in the universe and fear is the force that opposes love.

The question I want you to ask yourself as you begin to examine your spiritual beliefs or life philosophy is *"Do I experience the idea of God (the higher power in the universe) from a place of love or fear?"* This question is more important than you might realize. Your answer greatly affects the amount of peace you experience in your life and how you value yourself. Take a minute to ask yourself these questions:

- Is God (or the universe) a safe place for me or a scary place?
- Was I taught as a child to fear God?
- Was I told that God was keeping track of my mistakes and waiting to condemn me, or was I taught to see God as a source of unconditional love?
- Do I feel safe and valued by God?
- When I think about God, does it bring up feelings of inadequacy and shame, or safety and love?

You might be unsure about the true nature of God (or the life force in the universe) even if you have well defined religious beliefs. I say this because you might have been taught two conflicting ideas about God. You might have been consciously told God was love, but at the same time subconsciously taught that He might condemn you if you aren't good enough.

These two ideas don't mesh and cause a great deal of confusion for most people. Take a minute to think about what you were taught and what you currently believe.

Your policy about God being a safe place (or a scary place) affects every area of your life. It affects the way you interact with the world, feel about yourself, and treat other people. Take some time to explore your *feelings* about God, because they are clues about your subconscious beliefs. Remember that you could consciously see God as a safe place and still subconsciously fear Him. Your conscious and subconscious mind may not agree, and it is your subconscious beliefs that drive your feelings.

You might have also subconsciously projected some of your feelings about your earthly parents over to how you feel about God. This happens to most people to some degree. If your parents were involved, loving, and supportive, you can see God as involved, loving, and supportive. If your parents were distant, strict, or hard to please, you can see God as distant, strict, and hard to please, too. Did this happen to you?

You could also be projecting some of your own self-esteem issues *(your fears of not being good enough)* onto God. If you don't love yourself unconditionally, you may subconsciously believe that God doesn't love you unconditionally either. If you see yourself as inadequate, you may think that God sees you as inadequate. Your ideas about the nature of God might be nothing more than reflections of what you have experienced in your life. Catholic monk and author Thomas Merton said, "Our idea of God tells us more about ourselves than about Him." Consider the possibility that you have subconsciously created the nature of God in your own image, so to speak.

If you are experiencing God in a fear-based way and seeing Him as a threat, you are also seeing life as a test to prove your worth to God. If this has been your belief, *you are experiencing God through a foggy lens and you might want to rethink your perspective.*

I would like to suggest a fearless, love-based policy about the nature of God, the higher power in the universe. I hope you will at least consider how seeing God or this life force as the source of unconditional, perfect love might change how you feel about yourself and your life.

Troy's Story

Troy came to me for coaching because he was discouraged and angry. The last few years of his life had been very difficult and he felt worthless and alone. Troy wasn't alone, though. He had a wonderful wife and children who loved him. But he hadn't been very kind to them lately. His anger had driven some very selfish and mean behavior, and they were on the edge of leaving him.

The first thing I asked him about was his spiritual beliefs. He admitted he had been raised to see God as strict, uncaring, and judgmental. His parents had been very hard to please and had drilled into his head that he wasn't good enough. Now he was completely certain he would never measure up to anyone's standards, especially God's, so why try? He felt rejected and forgotten by God and had lost interest in trying to please Him.

In coaching, I helped Troy see that his entire perspective on God might have come from his parents' fears, and that none of it was necessarily accurate. I helped him see that he had the power to choose how he wanted to experience God. He admitted that his current belief system wasn't working for him and that he was open to the idea of changing his policy about the higher power.

This is the bottom line: You have no absolute proof of God's existence, and therefore no real proof of His true nature. This being the case, *you get to choose how you want to experience God.*

This is not only your right, but is an essential part of your free agency. You get to choose how you want to experience everything in your life, so you could choose to see God (the higher power in the universe) as the pure essence of perfect love if you want to. You have this power to see God as your safest place. You could believe that God, everything he does, and everything He thinks and feels about you are based in love, not fear, and that there is nothing whatsoever to fear about God (or the universe) or life.

You could believe that God knows who you are, sees the goodness in you, and loves you as you are right now. *This idea feels like truth to me.* I believe He knows what you've been through and why you made the choices you made, and does not judge you for those choices because He understands the lessons you needed to learn when you made them. I believe He knows your heart, your intentions, and your pain. I believe He also loves you unconditionally as you are right now in the same way you love your children wherever they are and no matter what they do. I believe He sent you here to learn and grow, not to be weeded out from among His "better" children. That idea is not consistent with the God of love whom I know.

I believe the higher power in the universe is compassionate, understanding, and all-knowing, and that there is nothing you can do that will change His love for you. I believe God's love for you is infinite and absolute, and your value as an irreplaceable, unique, one-of-a-kind, divine soul is infinite and absolute, too, because it is based in God's love for you.

Does this make sense to you the way it does to me? I believe this is truth. I believe your value is not on the line; that your value is literally absolute and unchangeable. You have the same infinite value no matter what you do or don't do. I believe you are a perfect and divine creation and as such your value is secure forever, no matter how many mistakes (driven by fear and misconception) you make. I believe God understands that your mistakes are part of your learning process. Mistakes teach you beautiful and important lessons. It doesn't make sense to condemn you for being lost, confused, scared, or stupid, when for the most part *we all are*. We are doing the best we can with what we know, but we don't know enough and are nowhere close to perfect. I believe God wants you to keep learning and growing, but that He loves you and accepts you as you are right now. I believe God wants you to understand the truth about all of this and experience joy. I believe you cannot find real meaning, purpose, or joy in life until you choose to trust these truths, accept your value as absolute, and see God as love.

Your mindset about the higher power in the universe is critically important because it affects your personal life and your business life. Seeing God as unconditional love drastically changes how you feel about yourself and how you treat other people. It removes your fear of not being good enough, which makes you more capable of loving and encouraging others. If God loves and values you unconditionally, then you are always good enough and there is nothing to fear. Seeing God in a love-based way can make you more productive, too, because you can waste a lot of time battling the fear of failure, and trust in God's absolute love for you can eliminate that fear and free you up to focus on other things. Think about this. *Fear has to be the opposite of God because it is the opposite of love.* Fear is selfish, needy, and focused on you. It doesn't make sense for God to want you to fear Him or your life.

It comes down to this: Either God wants you to live in fear of Him, always afraid you aren't good enough and focused on yourself, or He wants you to live in love, knowing you are safe and focused on loving other people. *Which feels more accurate to you?*

Take a minute, or a few days, to really think about this. (I'm not encouraging you to change religions by the way; I just want you to look at your religious doctrine or spiritual beliefs from a trust-and-love perspective.) If you have a set of religious or spiritual beliefs that is not taking away your fear of not being good enough, you might not understand your religion correctly.

I say this because all religions, accurately understood, will take away your fear of not being good enough. I believe there is a way to understand the tenets of *your religion*, right now, that will take away your fear and make you feel loved and safe. The problem is that no matter what you believe or to which religion you belong, there are two ways you can experience your beliefs. There is a fear way to experience your religion, and a love way to experience it. *All religions can be experienced both ways.* All life philosophies can be experienced both ways, too.

If you search your personal books of scripture, you will find both ideas equally represented. There are some verses or sections that validate a fear-based view of God and there are some that validate a love-based view of God. Don't be confused by this. Both ideas had to be represented for you to have free agency. Anything less than equal representation of each idea would take away your freedom to choose.

You get to choose how you want to experience everything in your life, including your religion. God will never force a mindset on you. Many of the people you know probably choose to experience your religion in a fear-based way. But you don't have to. You can choose to believe that you are unconditionally loved and see your value as infinite and absolute. Or you can continue to feel miserable and live in constant fear that you aren't good enough. It's up to you. *How do you want to live?*

Troy's Story continued:

Troy had to wrestle with this idea for a while before he understood that he was in control of how he experienced God and he therefore could choose to see Him in a different way. He realized that choosing to see God as love was a choice. Trusting God and His unconditional love for him was a choice. He could continue to distrust God and see Him as a threat if he wanted to, but it really didn't serve him to do so.

Troy decided to re-create his image of God into a higher power who kept him safe and loved him no matter what he did. He used his love for his own children to model his beliefs about God's love for him. He decided to trust in this love and let all his fears of not being good enough go. He wrote a new personal policy about God and read it daily. This changed everything.

Now it's your turn to do the same. Below is an example of my personal policy about the nature of God, the higher power in the universe. I strongly recommend that you process these ideas for a while and explore what feels like truth to you about God. Then take the time to write this very foundational policy for yourself. This policy is important because it greatly affects your life, your relationships, your business, and your general happiness in life. Feel free to use my example for ideas.

My Personal Policies about the Nature of God

This is my official policy about the nature of God (or the higher power in the universe):

God is love. That is a truth about which I am sure. He is my loving Heavenly Father and He wants me back no matter what.

As a parent, there is nothing my child could do that would make me reject him. I believe God is the source of all love, so there is no way that He is a less loving parent than I am.

He did not send me down here with a risk of losing me forever. God is a loving Father and He loves me perfectly, as I am right now. He knows my heart, He knows my potential, and He knows my great desire to be a good person. Nothing I do can change God's love for me. He wants me back no matter what — that is why He provided a Savior who made my journey here a safe one.

When I trust in God's love for me, it takes away my fear of not being good enough. This makes me more loving to the people in my life. This is what God wants for me. He wants me to experience love and share His love with the people around me. God is my safest place and I am in His loving hands all the time.

This is my policy about my religion, spiritual beliefs, and life philosophy:

There are many people who experience my religion from a place of fear. They have that choice because of free agency. The idea of fear is represented in scripture to give us a choice, but it is not what I choose. I choose to embrace living from a place of love for God, myself, and others. I choose to see my religion from a place of unconditional love, not from a place of fear. I choose to see God as love, and this journey through life as a safe place of learning. There is nothing to fear here. Every experience I have in my life is there to serve me and my process of learning. I am safely in God's hands the whole time.

He does not condemn or judge me. He only forgives and loves.

Take some time to write a new official policy about what you believe when it comes to your spiritual beliefs or life philosophy and the nature of God. Decide whether you are going to experience God and the universe as a safe and loving place, or something to fear. I believe changing this one policy could change how you feel about everything. It is that important.

Write a new policy that helps you clarify what you believe. If you are not sure what you believe yet, keep reading and exploring these ideas further before you write this important policy. You might need a greater understanding of love, trust, and fear first. Then come back and write this policy when you are ready.

I recommend you get a small notebook or journal and write "My Personal Policies and Procedures" on the front, write your new policies and procedures in that book, and read them often.

(The entire book is not about God and religion. It is just necessary to address these ideas at the beginning because of the affect they have on every other area of your life.)

3 – Who You Are

As an executive coach my first question for every new client is "Who are you?" I am always curious about their automatic unconscious answer, which usually ranges from their occupation to their role as a parent to their talents or their appearance. But none of these has anything to do with who they really are.

Gary's Story:

> Gary admitted from day one that he had no idea who he was anymore. He had always defined himself by his job, and since getting laid off he had completely lost his sense of identity. He was having trouble finding another job, and the longer he went unemployed the worse he felt about himself. Without a job he literally had no value. At least that is how it felt.

> I asked Gary to think about his personal spiritual beliefs and what he believed about his spirit or soul. These were things he had not explored before, at least not at that level. Who was he really? What was he created for? What was his purpose for being here? Did he believe in life after death? Was there more to his existence than just this world? If so, was his identity really based on his job?

Gary did have some spiritual beliefs about all of this, but he didn't see how those beliefs related to his current situation of being unemployed. He didn't see how clarifying his beliefs could help him create a healthy mindset about his value.

I explained to Gary that he could choose (if he wanted to) to get a sense of identity from his beliefs about his true worth instead of from his current situation. He could choose to let the enormous truth about his soul and the true nature of God (being love) determine his identity. If he believed God was love, he could choose to see himself as love, too.

I asked Gary to think about the times he felt the best about himself. He immediately described playing with his grandchildren, spending quality time with his wife, and doing charity work as his best moments. I explained to Gary that his love for life, his family, himself, God, and other people might be a better way to define himself. If his identity was based on his love, he could never lose it. He would be the same amazing, loving person no matter what was happening in his life or at work.

Gary decided to focus on being LOVE everywhere he went. He focused on being kinder and more tolerant of others. He looked for opportunities to lift and edify friends and family. He chose to focus on getting identity from his character instead of from his accomplishments. With this new identity he was more confident and attractive to employers, and he soon found a job.

Your love is who you are, too, but you probably don't identify yourself this way. You have probably worked your entire life to create a sense of identity around your job, your family, your hobbies, or your physical characteristics. But none of these is who you really are. You are not what you look like. You are not your family. You are not your job, income, or performance. You are not your current situation or the mistakes you have made. Mistakes are just locations on your journey; they have nothing to do with who you are, and neither does what you do or how successful you are.

You are bigger than all those things. You are much more than just a businessman or a mom or a student. You are a divine, irreplaceable, one-of-a-kind, amazing, loving, eternal being, and your value comes from that fact alone. You come from God, who is love, which to me means that you are love, too. You have to be. And if you are love, nothing you do or don't do can change your value because no matter what you do or how many mistakes you make, you are still YOU; you are still LOVE. You can't help it. You cannot be anything else.

It also means that your value is so big, amazing, divine, momentous, and eternal that it overrides any mistakes, circumstances, or situations in your life. The situations in your life have nothing at all to do with who you are. They will all pass away, but you will go on forever. You have the option of seeing yourself this way if you want to.

If you are having a hard time getting your head around this concept, keep reading anyway and keep thinking about what would change if you formed your sense of identity around being love.

....

clarity**point**: **You are a divine, eternal being, and your value is infinite and absolute.** You are an irreplaceable, incomparable soul in a process of becoming, and your value comes from that fact alone.

....

Think about the last time you showed up with love to lift, help, or serve another person. How did you feel in that moment? You felt wonderful... because you were being the real you. You were being love. It always feels wonderful to be who you are.

When you really get this concept, you will stop trying to impress people with your clothes, your appearance, your property, your paycheck, or your job, and you will focus on being love instead. It's actually the only thing about you people really care about. So every morning I do my best to get dressed in something nice, then I put all thoughts about my appearance and performance aside and go get them with my love.

You are a divine, irreplaceable, one-of-a-kind soul, and there is no other achievement, title, or role that is more meaningful than that. Your qualities and attributes and how you treat other people are the only things about who you are that really matter.

Take some time to really think about how being love and letting your value come from that quality alone could change your sense of self-worth. Could you be a successful business person, a dedicated student, or a busy mom while focused on being a force of love? What would that look like?

Before you write your policy, here's an example, here's an example of my personal policy to help you. Think about what might change in your life if you chose to see yourself this way. When you are ready, write a personal policy about who you are.

My Personal Policy about Who I Am

I am love.

I am my love for God, life, other people, and myself.

I am meant to be an expression of God's love in this world and to share my love with everyone I can. I am my highest, best self when I choose to behave with love. I have stopped trying to earn approval or a sense of identity from what I look like and what I do. Everywhere I go, I get them with my love. Love is the essence of who I am, and it is my purpose for being here. I am not my appearance, my weight, or my accomplishments. I am not my clothes, my car, or my job. At the end of the day the only thing that matters is my love for the people in my life. I experience joy when I remember this. I am love.

Now it's your turn. Please take the time to write your own personal policy about who you are in your notebook. Officially declare that you will not define yourself by what you do or where you are; you will focus on the essence of your being instead.

4 – How You Think

For you to have the freedom to choose how you want to live, you must have at least two options all the time. We already established there are two opposing forces in the universe, a love force and a fear force; that same dynamic must exist everywhere.

If you are love (because that is the core of your being), there has to be something inside your head that is part of you but that opposes your love, so that you have the opportunity to choose.

I call the opposing or shadow force in your head your *ego* or the Voice of Fear. This voice is like a little devil sitting on your shoulder, constantly encouraging scared, immature, selfish, unloving behavior. I believe this Voice of Fear was required for you to have a full good-and-evil education here. I was raised to think of this voice as my carnal-nature or natural-man side. Some people refer to it as their inner-critic or lower-self side. You should choose a name that makes sense to you based on your personal beliefs. For simplicity's sake, in this book I refer to it as the Voice of Fear.

You can start paying attention to your thoughts today and see if you can recognize thoughts that might be coming from your Voice of Fear side. If you become more aware of these thoughts, you will then have the opportunity to consciously reject them and replace them with trust-and-love-based thoughts. But if you continue to let them unconsciously drive your life without recognizing their source, you won't have power over them.

Remember that the real you – *your spirit or your love side* – also has a voice in your head. When you consciously choose to listen to this voice you can override fear and behave like the person you are meant to be. In this book I refer to this voice as your Voice of Truth, and it is the real, eternal, divine, loving, spirit part of you that cannot be diminished by anything or anyone because its value is infinite and absolute. The Voice of Truth is also inseparably connected to universal truth, whereas the Voice of Fear in your head tells lies; it tells you that you aren't good enough, while the truth-and-love part of you knows you *can't* be "not good enough" because your value isn't even on the line. The Voice of Truth, by the way, is the real YOU.

clarity**point:** **You have a "Voice of Truth" that is your spirit or soul.** It is the source of your trust and love. It is the real you.

Read through the chart below that compares the Voice of Fear to the Voice of Truth. *(You might want to mark this page and refer to this chart often to help you choose how you want to experience each moment.)* When you listen to the Voice of Truth, you will feel safe and loved. You will have the ability to see other people accurately as divine, amazing, irreplaceable human beings in the process, just like you. You will have the ability to forgive them and live in wisdom and compassion. You can do this because all of these qualities are in you. In fact, they are who you really are.

Voice of Fear	**Voice of Truth**
ego	spirit
fear and doubt	trust and love
foggy	clarity
all about me	love for self and others
must earn value	value is infinite
insecure	confident
I'm not good enough	my value is absolute
lack – fear of loss	abundance–trust
criticism	forgiveness
sees others as different from you	sees others as the same as you
focused on getting	focused on wholeness
not accurate	truth

The Voice of Fear in your head has another agenda, though. Its job is to distract you from trust and love. It wants to prevent you from feeling safe so you will stay focused on yourself and can't focus on loving people. It wants you to be needy and insecure. It tries to make you forget who you really are and doubt your value, and undermines your trust in the process of life. It has been working tirelessly your whole life to keep you here – *has it been working?*

If this voice is driving most of the time, it is the primary reason you aren't happy and are struggling with self-esteem. But do not worry. *I am going to give you all the tools you need to change this.*

The first step, though, is to recognize that you have a choice and claim the power to choose. Dr. Frankl said:

> In the concentration camps, in this living laboratory and on this testing ground, we watched and witnessed some of our comrades behave like swine while others behaved like saints. Man has both potentials within himself; which one is actualized depends on decisions but not on conditions.[2]

In the Harry Potter series (which I bring up here in honor of my children), J. K. Rowling wrote, *"It is our choices that show what we truly are, far more than our abilities."*

Read this wonderful exchange between Harry and Sirius Black. Harry says, "What if after everything that I've been through, something's gone wrong inside me? What if I'm becoming bad?"

"I want you to listen to me very carefully, Harry. You're not a bad person. You're a very good person, who bad things have happened to. Besides, the world isn't split into good people and [bad people]. We've all got both light and dark inside us. What matters is the part we choose to act on. That's who we really are."

This is truth. You get to decide who you will be, which side you will listen to, and how you will experience each moment of your life. *The moments and the situations don't define you; your choices do,* and you always have these same two options in every moment. You can experience this moment in fear, focused on yourself, or you can experience it in trust and love. It's up to you. **BUT** (and this is a big *but*), if you don't consciously choose to experience this moment in trust and love, your subconscious mind will choose for you, and it will probably choose fear, since fear is probably your autopilot. *(This is a key principle so I am repeating it often on purpose.)*

Roger's Story:

> Roger was suffering with a huge fear of failure and some serious low self-esteem when he came to me for coaching. As a child, he had experienced a great deal of abuse and had spent years in therapy to deal with his past and his feelings of worthlessness. But negative self-talk was still running his life. He was constantly afraid of failing and being hurt by other people, and all this noise in his head was driving him crazy.
>
> It took some work in coaching to convince Roger that he had the power to change his attitude toward himself; that

it was in his control. He laughed when I suggested that he just trust his value was infinite and absolute (and not on the line) and that he was good enough as he was. It couldn't be that easy.

His negative programming was very strong, and overcoming it and choosing trust when those negative thoughts showed up would be a battle. But the more we talked about it he could see that he did have that choice in every moment. He didn't have to let his Voice of Fear drive. He could choose to replace its lies with truth. He could override negative self-talk in each specific moment if he wanted to.

He found it really helped when he started seeing the Voice of Fear as a little demon on his shoulder. He even called it that and told it to shut up often. Separating himself from the Voice of Fear and negativity made a big difference. It wasn't him who thought he was worthless; it was that little demon on this shoulder. The little demon was a smart one, though. It used all the horrible things that were said to him over the years against him. But he could override it. He had the power to say "Thank you for your input but I'm not going there anymore. I know my real value!"

It took some time of committed effort to take control of his head, and on occasion the demon still tries to pull Roger down. But he now knows what to do in those moments and is winning the war.

You have the power to choose trust and love and override your Voice of Fear, too. You can choose to see your value as infinite and absolute in any moment. But if you don't fight and claim your power to choose – if you deny that power or give it away to other people or situations and let them determine your value – *that is also a choice.* Remember, if you don't consciously choose trust and love, you are unconsciously choosing fear.

clarity**point**:   **If you don't consciously choose trust and love in each moment, your subconscious policies will choose for you, and they usually choose fear.**

Your subconscious mind is dangerous because it moves very quickly. It makes you react and feel a certain way (usually negative) before you even have time to think. Because your subconscious policies of fear happen so fast, you will have to pay close attention to catch them and replace them with truth in time.

Start watching out for any thoughts or feelings that are immature, angry, inaccurate, selfish, weak, scared, dramatic, or in any way based in fear. In those moments, start to practice consciously choosing love for yourself and others instead. It will be a challenge at first, but you can do it. It will help immensely if you will create a personal policy about the Voice of Fear and the Voice of Truth.

Remember that every thought that shows up in your head is coming from one of those two voices. You must decide how you will listen for and manage their advice. Take some time to define your two sides and what you are going to call them. Here are my personal policies to get you started:

My Personal Policies about My Two Sides

This is my policy about the Voice of Fear in my head and how it affects me:

I am here to learn and grow. I have been given free agency to facilitate my learning process. In order to exercise free agency, there have to be choices. This means there has to be a force in my head that opposes my love. Fear is that force.

Upon arriving here on earth, I took on a Voice of Fear or ego side. This voice is not who I am. It is in my head to provide opposition to my love and give me the opportunity to figure out who I am and how I want to live.

Fear shows up in my life on a daily basis. I have to watch out for fear-based thoughts because they encourage me to be selfish, immature, and dramatic. I am aware of how and why this happens. Fear is trying to distract me from being who I really am – love. It is trying to undermine my trust in God and life. I clearly understand fear's purpose and I will not allow it to distance me from my true nature. I choose to focus on giving love to other people in every situation. This drives away my fear because it cannot exist where there is love.

This is my policy about my Voice of Truth:

I have two sides, but the divine, eternal, one-of-a-kind, irreplaceable spirit side is who I really am. I call this side my Voice of Truth. This side is divine because I am a child of divinity. Because of this side, I am capable of seeing situations and people the way God sees them, with love, accuracy, and compassion. I want this side to drive my life. In every situation I ask my Inner Truth what I should do. I immediately know I should respond with trust and love. The Voice of Truth reminds me that I am always good enough, and helps me live with love and peace.

This is my policy about choosing how I feel and experience every situation in my life:

I have the power to choose my attitude, mindset, and reaction to every situation. I do not give that power away. I consciously choose to respond in trust about my value and with love towards myself and others in every situation. I trust God and the process of my life. I know that He loves me and created this beautiful and sometimes difficult journey to serve me. Even when things are hard, I trust this. I am committed to consciously choosing my attitude in every moment.

Now it's your turn. Spend some time writing your new policies on your two sides and your power to choose your thoughts.

5 – What's the Point?

Now that you have decided on some policies regarding your spiritual beliefs and who you are, it is important that you clarify the purpose and point of your life. *Do you have a clearly defined purpose for your life?* Have you thought about why you are here and what the point of the journey is?

Over the years I have had the privilege of working with people from almost every corner of the planet. I have asked each of them about the purpose of their life. Though there were differences in personal meaning, every one of them, regardless of their religion or life philosophy, had a similar ultimate purpose. We all innately seem to know we are here to LEARN and LOVE.

We are all innately driven by something deep inside us to constantly improve ourselves, learn, grow, develop our talents, and improve our character throughout our lives. We seem to know that this life is a process of becoming the best version of ourselves we can be. Self-improvement seems to be a natural part of our being.

We are also innately driven to help and serve other people along our way. We subconsciously desire to be an expression of our love. Most people who discover a personal mission in life find that mission in helping others. Dr. Frankl believed that the human soul's highest need was self-transcendence – *finding a purpose larger than one's self* – and that that purpose usually meant making a positive difference in the lives of other people. Because of this I believe we are here to learn and love.

Because these two ideas resonate as truth with almost everyone, I have come to believe that they are universal principles of truth. I also believe that we are specifically here *to learn to love.* This means, first and foremost, that we are here to learn to forgive ourselves and other people.

. . . .

clarity**point:**   **The purpose and point of this life is to learn and love – and it may be more specifically to learn to love.**

. . . .

If you will consider making learning and loving your ultimate purpose and official policy, it will drastically change how you experience your life at home and at work. With this perspective you will see each situation in terms of what it is here to teach you or who it is giving you an opportunity to love (and more specifically how that situation could teach you to love at a deeper level).

Could you step back from your current challenge right now and look at it from this perspective? What is it here to teach you? Who are you meant to forgive? Think about this for a minute.

Even though life is difficult at times, you must understand that these challenges are not here to beat you, defeat you, or squash you like a bug. Life is not against you (even though it feels that way sometimes). Every single experience is in your life to *serve your process of growth and learning*. Every situation you experience serves that purpose and is ultimately for your good.

This doesn't mean you will enjoy every situation, though; the learning process here on earth includes some very painful and discouraging experiences. But you can lessen the suffering by looking for meaning and purpose. Even Dr. Frankl, who was very familiar with suffering, said that suffering would cease or at least lessen if you could see meaning and purpose behind it. When you see meaning behind your experiences – *that they facilitate growth* – then they count for something. And an attitude of trust and seeing your personal trials as a perfect part of your process of becoming will always serve you, especially since the only other option is fear, bitterness, and anger, and those emotions don't serve you at all.

But, you can choose to see life as a random, meaningless set of accidents if you want to. You can choose to deny meaning and purpose and live in fear of loss that your life won't be good enough. But you will end up spending most of your energy trying to protect yourself and you won't experience much joy or peace. As a matter of fact you will experience a lot of unnecessary suffering. But you certainly have the option of living that way if you want to.

Karrie's Story

Karrie was grieving the loss of her beautiful teenaged daughter to suicide. Over the last few years, dealing with this grief had taken a huge toll on her physically and emotionally. She was having a hard time getting out of bed in the morning and even caring about anything or anyone.

The first time we spoke, I asked her what she thought the purpose of her life here was. Her first answer (which came from her subconscious programming) was "to suffer." When I suggested that life might have a little more meaning than that, she frankly couldn't see it. I explained that most people innately feel we are here to learn and that our experiences serve our process of growth. She agreed to consider this idea as truth and at least play around with it. We discussed at great length the lessons she had learned about life, love, and people through this horrific experience. She could see ways the experience had made her more compassionate and wise than she had been before.

During our discussions she realized that she really had only two options when it came to looking at this experience: she could see her loss as meaningless, brutal suffering that served no one, or she could see it as meaningful and serving the purpose of making them all better and wiser. Either way she was going to suffer, but the latter did feel better.

She did not believe God had made this horrible thing happen, though. Karrie believed her daughter had chosen this path to teach her important lessons she needed to learn. She chose to believe that she, too, had signed up for this experience because of the amazing lessons it could facilitate in her life. Through this experience she was gaining an astounding depth of love and understanding for people and their suffering. This had changed her. She was learning to love at a whole new level.

She struggled a bit with the idea that her journey was the perfect journey for her, because it had been far from perfect. But she understood that it had probably been the right journey for her even though it was difficult.

In the end, Karrie could see that choosing to embrace this experience as a divine and meaningful process of becoming gave her some peace and allowed her to move forward in life. She also found purpose in being a beacon of hope, love, and friendship for the people around her. She decided to focus on being love and trusting life.

Your life is the perfect learning process for you, too, and there are no accidents. Every experience you have is your perfect next lesson for some reason. But just to clarify, I am not talking about predestination here. I believe you have free agency and choose the path your life will follow moment by moment. This means the creation of your life (your perfect learning process) is happening as you live it. Every minute of every day you and the universe are co-creating your life and the lives of the people around you. But you always get to choose your next best lesson. If you make a bad choice, you apparently needed the lesson that choice provided. Because the universe knows you and what you need, it throws some lessons into the mix, too. (Occasionally you get a lesson you don't remember signing up for.) But understand that the purpose behind it is to help you learn to love at a deeper level. When you trust this, you experience more happiness and less fear.

- -

clarity**point**: **Your life is a perfect and divine process of learning and growth.** You are safe in this process because the objective is for your good. Every situation in your life is there to serve you in some way.

- -

Take some time and at least consider making learning and loving *(and learning to love)* your official purpose. Trust me that this is an important part of the path to fearlessness. You must have a clearly defined purpose that gives meaning to your life and everything you experience. Take the time to write a personal policy about why you are here. This will help you see your experiences more accurately. Here is my personal policy to give you some ideas:

My Personal Policy about the Purpose of Life

I am here to learn and love. This journey through life is a divine process of growth to help me become the best version of myself I can be. I am also here to love and be an expression of love in this world. I believe ultimately I am here to learn to love.

I keep this purpose in mind daily. In every situation I ask myself, "What is this experience here to teach me? How can it help me learn to love at a deeper level?" This gives meaning and purpose to my life.

Every moment of every day, with every choice I make, God, the universe, and I are creating my perfect journey of growth and learning. Everything that happens to me facilitates this process. I trust the process of my life because it is all for my good. The universe knows exactly what lesson I need next. I trust God and this process.

God and the universe know what they're doing.

I get to decide how I want to experience each situation in my life. I can experience it in fear or I can trust the process and experience love. It is totally up to me. I keep the true purpose of my life in mind all the time.

What is your personal policy about the purpose of life? Think about making learning and loving your purpose; it will change the way you experience everything. Go to your notebook and write it now.

6 – Classroom or Test?

Now that you have clarified your purpose for being here (to learn and love) and the force opposing that purpose (the Voice of Fear), the next questions you must answer are:

1. What is the nature of this life?

2. Is this journey a safe one or is failing a possibility?

3. What if you don't learn enough?

4. What if you struggle to show up with love?

5. Can you get off course or fail?

6. How can you know if you're good enough?

7. What does "good enough" even mean?

These questions create confusion for most people, even those with strong, well-defined religious beliefs. You might have been taught one thing but subconsciously feel another. You might have been taught that your journey through life is a safe one because you can repent from your mistakes, be forgiven, and try again, and that your mistakes won't count against you. If you believe this life should feel safe, this belief should take away your fear of not being good enough.

The problem is that depending on your religion you might have also been given a long list of things you need to do to earn forgiveness. You might subconsciously feel that you have to be almost perfect to be good enough or qualify. You may have been taught to see life as a test and that there is a good chance you won't pass. This would make your journey feel unsafe, and totally contradicts the other idea you were taught.

Take a minute to really think about what you were taught and how your life feels. Which of these ideas has been driving your subconscious feelings about life? Has life *felt* like a test where your value is constantly on the line and you might not measure up? Or has it *felt* like a classroom, a safe place to learn and grow?

It is critically important that you figure out what you want to believe about the nature of life, because it greatly affects your self-esteem, your attitude, and the amount of happiness you experience.

If the purpose of life is really to learn and love (and learn to love), you might think of life as the experience of being sent off to college. You are here (in earth school) to learn and eventually move on to the next sphere, which would be your graduation. The question is what kind of school is this? *Is it a testing center or a classroom?*

If life is a testing center, then every day is a test and every test counts towards your final grade. If life is a testing center, you are here to *prove* your value through your performance, and too many mistakes can mean you fail. In a testing center your mistakes deserve punishment and even rejection. If life is a test, your value is constantly on the line.

If life is a classroom, your mistakes don't count towards your final grade. If life is a classroom, you're still in the learning process part, in which if you make a mistake you can just erase it and try again. In a classroom your mistakes deserve course correction and education, not punishment. Here the goal is to teach you how to behave better, not to fail you or get rid of you. In a classroom you can be a work in progress, and that's okay.

In a classroom you are free to make mistakes in order to learn, because mistakes are part of learning. There are still consequences to every choice, but in a classroom you can't fail because *your value isn't on the line.* If life is a classroom, you have the same value no matter how much you struggle, how many mistakes you make, or how you perform. If life is a classroom, you are safe and therefore free to focus on other people.

If you have subconsciously experienced life as a testing center, you have been living with much more fear and anxiety than necessary and you haven't been seeing anything in your life accurately. *Seeing life as a testing center fogs your lens more than any other subconscious policy.* It puts your value in question with everything you do. But you do not have to live this way. You do not have to see life as a test anymore. You can change your official policy and choose to see life as a classroom, and I highly recommend you do this. It will make your life much happier.

. . . .

clarity**point**:   **A fear-based philosophy about life (seeing life as a testing center) can prevent you from seeing yourself and situations accurately.**
A fear of failing skews your perspective and distracts you from learning and loving.

. . . .

You can change your policy right now and officially see your life as a classroom within the framework of your current religion or life philosophy. You have the right to see your spiritual beliefs this way. It is, in fact, the way they are meant to be seen. I know this because there is no way a higher power would want you to live with a fear of failing hanging over your head. There is nothing about fear that serves your purpose for being here. You are here to learn, and a fear of failing prevents you from learning. You are here to love, and fear is the force that opposes love and encourages selfishness. *The higher power in the universe would never want you to spend your life afraid that you aren't good enough, and focused on yourself.*

This change in mindset will change the way you feel about your past mistakes, too. You are here to learn, and learning required those mistakes. Mistakes facilitated some of your most amazing lessons. It would make no sense to punish you for the very mistakes that you are here to experience to teach you the perfect lessons you were meant to learn, right?

Remember the conditions under which you arrived here. You came here with amnesia, knowing nothing, literally as dumb as dirt. You arrived in a family who, even if they were fantastic, were imperfect, struggling, scared students in the classroom of life, too. Your parents most likely didn't know enough to teach you what you needed to know. Then life threw difficulty after difficulty at you, and you have done the best you could with what you knew. But let's be honest; it's been messy. Declaring you a failure or not good enough when the journey has been this tough would be like failing a kindergartener because they didn't understand college calculus. It wouldn't make sense.

To create more happiness and success in your life, you must change your policy about the nature of life and officially choose to see it as a classroom, not a test. You can make the conscious choice to see life as a classroom right now, if you want to. But the universe will not force this mindset (policy) on you. *You get to choose how you want to live.* If you want to experience fear that you aren't good enough and kick against the pricks every day trying to earn your value and avoid failing, you are more than welcome to. Some people seem to like the fear concept and believe it motivates them. But you don't have to see your life that way. You can be just as motivated by trust and love. (Later in the book I will teach you how love motivation really works.)

Before you write a personal policy on the nature of life, though, think about this concept for a while and what feels like truth to you. Would a higher power really send you into this messy, painful classroom with the deck stacked against you and expect you to pass all the tests? Some of you have had a really difficult journey here. Some of you were raised by parents who seriously messed you up. I find it hard to believe that God doesn't understand the reality of your situation and see that you are a good person even if you made a whole lot of mistakes.

* *

clarity**point**: **You can choose to see your journey as a classroom without the fear of failure.** Or you can choose to live in fear and see it as a test. It's up to you.

* *

Now, just because life's a classroom and your value isn't on the line doesn't mean you should go out and make bad choices without concern for the consequences. *That would not create the life you want.* You should continue to do your best and make good, smart, honest, caring choices, but you should do it for YOU, so you can create a happy and successful life. Don't do it out of obligation or fear of punishment. *Fear is not necessary to motivate you to be a good person*; you can do good things because you love people, yourself, and life. You can make good choices because you desire the good results good choices create. This is how you can live when you live without fear.

You are here on this amazing journey through life to experience every dimension of the human condition (including mistakes, failures, shame, and guilt). Failure experiences, which you will surely have on occasion, are a critical part of your education, but again, they do not affect your value because your value isn't on the line. Your value isn't on the line because life's a classroom, not a test. Your failures are just locations on your journey; they are classes you got signed up for, but they have nothing to do with who you are and they do not affect your value.

If you are struggling to accept this concept (that you have nothing to fear) as truth, you are not alone. Many people have been taught their whole lives to see life as a test and expect condemnation and punishment for their mistakes. They want to accept these love-based ideas as truth, but they are scared to.

Are you scared to believe that you have nothing to fear? Are you afraid that without a fear of failing or going to hell you wouldn't be motivated to do the right things?

You need to rethink this belief, because fear doesn't serve you, and if you do good things only because you fear punishment or rejection if you don't, does it really count? *Think about it.* Are they real choices or are you being held hostage?

I believe that a good choice doesn't serve you if you feel forced to make it; if it wasn't what you wanted or how you really felt, then you didn't really choose it. The famous cultural anthropologist and writer Margaret Mead said, "It is an open question whether any behavior based on fear of eternal punishment can be regarded as ethical or should be regarded as merely cowardly." For your choice to count and mean something, you must be loved and safe either way.

Another common misconception about fear is that being afraid you're not good enough is righteous or humble behavior. Some people think self-deprecation (seeing yourself as not good enough) is a righteous state because it is humble. Do not confuse fear of not being good enough with humility. Being afraid you aren't good enough has nothing to do with being humble.

Author C. S. Lewis wrote a beautiful and accurate definition of humility: *"Humility is not thinking less of yourself... it is thinking of yourself less."* It is about feeling safe so you can focus on other people. It is not about being in fear and seeing yourself as worthless!

So be a good person, do good things, learn, and love other people, but do these things because you love yourself, God, life, and people, not because you fear going to hell if you don't. Keep the commandments (or whatever tenets you believe) because you want to be happy. *Do it for you.* God and the universe will love you unconditionally no matter which path you choose. You can learn whatever lessons you choose for yourself. If you want to learn things the hard way and experience fear, guilt, and shame, that is okay. But nothing you do (or don't do) can separate you from love.

Are you ready to accept this truth and let it take away your fear of not being good enough? I hope so.

Sheila's Story

Sheila had a hard time accepting the idea that her journey was a safe process of growth. She had been taught as a kid to see life as a testing center, and that had always been her subconscious policy. She honestly thought the purpose of life was to be tested, and because of this belief she was constantly afraid she wasn't good enough.

Her parents had used fear, shame, and guilt to motivate their children. While this approach did motivate Shelia to some degree, it also created serious self-esteem issues. She believed she had to be nearly perfect or she was totally worthless. No matter what Sheila did, she never felt good enough. The crazy part was that she should have felt amazing about who she was. She was a very smart, talented woman. She had raised a healthy, happy family and had a successful career. Still, she felt like a failure because she wasn't perfect enough.

Sheila knew something had to change. She was not happy and her negative attitude was taking a toll on her family and co-workers. She started to see how she was confused about the process of life. She saw life as being against her and literally setting her up to fail. The more Sheila thought about these old policies, the more she realized they didn't make sense.

She decided to write a new policy making life a classroom, not a testing center. This fit perfectly with her spiritual beliefs. She knew if she could change her policy about life, she could live with less fear and focus more on learning and loving. She also realized that life would be more enjoyable that way. Over the next year everything in her life got better. Because she felt more secure, she focused more on showing up for other people. She created less drama in her relationships and started to find joy at work.

Changing this one policy changed everything for Sheila.

I encourage you to consider seeing life as a classroom instead of a test and see how that feels to you. Having a clearly defined policy about the nature of life and seeing life as a classroom instead of a test is, I believe, the most powerful policy you can make, because it changes how you feel about everything else. Here is an example of my personal policy about this:

My Personal Policy about the Nature of Life

My life is a perfect process of growth and learning made just for me. God, the universe, and I co-create my perfect journey every day with every choice I make, every second of the day. My life is a classroom, not a testing center, and my value is not on the line here. I am a divine, amazing, struggling, scared student in the classroom of life, doing the best I can with what I know. I allow myself to be a work in progress, and because life is a classroom I know my mistakes don't affect my value. My value isn't on the line here at all.

Because life is a classroom, every experience is here to teach me something and facilitate my growth. Every person in my life is a teacher and every mistake is a lesson. When I make a mistake, I do not waste time in guilt or shame. I learn from the mistake, erase it, and try again. I focus on correcting what I didn't know. I strive to make good choices because I want to live abundantly and become the best person I can be.

Humility is not about thinking less of myself; it is about thinking of myself less. I know that I am a divine, amazing, spiritual being and that my value is infinite and absolute. I am here to learn and grow. I am here to be a force for love in the world. I focus on loving other people everywhere I go.

Go to your notebook and create your own personal policy about the nature of life. Make sure you are clear about how seeing life as a classroom affects your self-worth.

7 – Your Real Value

It is time you knew the truth about who you are, especially since your Voice of Fear is working so hard to convince you that you aren't good enough. The truth is that you are an amazing, divine, irreplaceable, one-of-a-kind soul with incredible gifts and talents, but you don't remember how amazing you are because upon arriving here you developed a bad case of amnesia. I believe this was a crucial part of your classroom experience because it gave you the opportunity to decide who you wanted to be. It gave you the opportunity to decide how you will determine your own worth, and that is one of your main responsibilities here. *You are in charge of your self-esteem.*

Unfortunately, you have not been claiming the power to determine your own value. You have been giving this power away to situations and other people, allowing them to judge you. I recommend you change this and rethink the entire system you have been using to determine your worth.

You are an irreplaceable, one-of-a-kind, amazing being. There will never be another you, and this fact alone makes you infinitely and absolutely valuable. Having absolute value means you cannot be diminished by anything or anyone.

You are bulletproof and nothing can change your value. You are also a struggling, scared student in the classroom of life, participating in a divine process of learning and growth. And you don't have to be perfect to be right on track. Giving yourself permission to be imperfect, and still valuable, means you will quickly forgive yourself your mistakes and see them accurately as lessons.

In this chapter you will have the opportunity to write a new policy about your true value and commit to letting this policy override what other people think about you, any results you get, and the outcome of any work you do. You must know *with every fiber of your being* that nothing can diminish your value because your value isn't changeable. You must refuse to let anyone take this truth away from you ever again.

If you write a new policy along these lines and adopt it as your core belief, it will change your life. It will change your life because low self-esteem is the root cause of most of your problems. When you don't feel good about yourself, it negatively affects your relationships, your performance at work, and your behavior towards other people. You cannot perform at your best with the core fear of not being good enough in the way. It keeps you too focused on you.

clarity**point**: **Low self-esteem (the fear that you aren't good enough) is the root cause of most problems.**

Your self-esteem is also a one-person job. You must eliminate the fear of not being good enough and choose to value yourself accurately for yourself and by yourself. No one can repair your self-esteem for you. Your spouse cannot fix it. Your parents cannot fix it. Your boss cannot fix it. No amount of success or beauty enhancements can fix it. *You have to fix it by changing the way you see yourself.* You have to choose to see yourself accurately, see life as a classroom, and commit to the policy that you have the same value no matter how you perform. It is time to claim the power to do this once and for all.

When you value yourself accurately, other people will feel your rock-solid confidence and see you as valuable, too. But if you don't do this, and continue to let situations, subconscious programs, and other people determine your value, other people will feel that too, and they will subconsciously lose respect for you.

clarity**point**: **You are the one responsible for your self-esteem. You are the one who must choose to value yourself accurately.**

clarity**point**: **No one can see your value unless you believe it first.**

Your value is unchangeable and absolute, and this means you are totally safe all the time. No one can hurt you or diminish you without your permission. The problem is that the Voice of Fear doesn't want you to feel safe. It wants you to think that your flaws, mistakes, and less-than-perfect features diminish your value in a permanent way all the time. But they don't. They don't affect your value at all. They have nothing to do with your value. (At least you have the option of seeing yourself this way if you want to.)

Imagine a sweet, puffy, glazed doughnut sitting on a plate in front of you. Does the fact that this doughnut has a hole in the middle take away from its value? After all, something is missing. But does the fact that something is missing make the doughnut inadequate or not good enough?

Of course it doesn't. The hole does not diminish the value of the doughnut because doughnuts are supposed to have holes. The hole is a perfect part of a perfect doughnut. *A perfect doughnut always has something missing.*

You are very much like that doughnut. You have wonderful goodness about you but you also have some holes. I'm talking about your mistakes, flaws, and less-than-perfect features. But these holes do not take away from your value either. They are a perfect part of the whole you. You wouldn't be the same you without them. Doughnuts and people are supposed to have things missing. We aren't meant to be perfect and we don't have to be perfect to have infinite value.

Mistakes and flaws just make you human. They make you real and they actually help you connect with other people. They give you empathy and compassion for others' flaws and faults. They make you less judgmental and more kind. Your flaws and weaknesses are not "good things"; granted they are things you will keep working to overcome, *but they don't take away from your infinite and absolute value because nothing can.* That is what *infinite* and *absolute* mean. As I wrote above, you can choose fear and see your flaws as taking away from your value if you want to. You have that choice. The universe will not force you to see yourself accurately.

The truth is that you are magnificent, irreplaceable, and incomparable as you are right now. Even though there are things you don't like about yourself, and you have some faults, and you have made some mistakes along the way, there are many more good things about you to appreciate. If you are having a hard time seeing your goodness through the seemingly huge flaws blocking your view, chances are you have even more love and goodness inside you than most people.

Let me explain why. The Voice of Fear must provide equal opposition to your love. So if your Voice of Fear is working really hard to convince you that you're not good enough, it is because you are a really loving, amazing person; the Voice of Fear doesn't want you to discover that. If you knew how amazing you were, you might use your gifts to make a difference in the world. It doesn't want this. It wants you to stay focused on your fear of not being good enough instead.

Could this be happening to you right now? Has that Voice of Fear in your head worked your whole life to keep you focused on your faults, flaws, and a fear of failure? Remember its agenda. It wants you to stay focused on your less-than-perfect features so that you will be too distracted to be a force for love in the world.

You cannot let this happen. You are meant to live with more joy and more love than you are currently living with.

Don's Story

Don came to me with low self-esteem and suffering from serious depression. He was in counseling for depression, but he was not making much progress changing his self-esteem. Despite the fact that he was an amazing person who was very intelligent and had a gift for understanding people, he still felt inadequate all the time. Don was very critical of his weight and he had let his weight determine his value for most of his life.

After a few weeks of coaching, a different man began to emerge. Don started to see his real infinite value. He decided to write some new policies about being bulletproof, infinite, and absolute. He decided to write a policy officially declaring that his mistakes did not affect his value; nor did his weight or how he performed at work. When he chose to see his value as unchangeable, it changed everything.

Don also started to consciously hear the negative Voice of Fear that was trying to keep him afraid all the time. He learned how to replace his fear-based thoughts with trust-

and-love-based ones (something I'm going to teach you to do, too). He started to reach out to other people more and look for opportunities to serve them.

Don even started seeing the challenges in his life differently. He could see that every terrible thing that had happened to him (even being overweight) had served him in some way. Every flaw had made him more understanding and empathetic to other people and their struggles. He still wanted to lose some weight and get healthier, but he could now do so from a place of joy rather than shame. He could lose the weight to feel better, not to prove his value.

Now everywhere he goes Don is on a mission to lift and love other people. His policy – to focus on other people instead of his flaws – is changing his life completely. He is too busy being a force for love to worry about not being good enough anymore.

Now it's your turn. Your value is not affected by what you look like either. It is not affected by your dress size, your income level, or how well you perform at what you do. It is not affected by what people think of you, how clean your house is, how much money you make, or how you compare to other people. As a matter of fact, it is not affected by your performance or your assets at all.

Situations such as being underemployed, divorced, single, struggling with addiction, overweight, failing, depressed, or stuck are just locations on your journey through life. They are not who you are.

Think of it this way... if you were on a cross-country road trip, you might have to drive through Texas. Texas is a large state and it might take you quite a while to drive through. You might even have some car trouble and get stuck in Texas for a little while. During that time, does being in Texas make you a Texan?

Of course not, it is just a location on your journey. *It has nothing to do with who you are.* You made the decision to drive through Texas, and you will probably learn some important lessons from the trip, but it doesn't affect your value or change *who* you are.

Whatever situations you have been through or are going through in your life, they are just locations on your journey. They are classes you got signed up for in your perfect classroom journey. Some classes (experiences) you sign yourself up for through the choices you make, and sometimes the universe signs you up for a class. But these experiences do not affect your value either way. *They are just lessons.* Your value comes from your love. Your value comes from the fact that you are a divine, infinite, and amazing being. These attributes are who you are.

clarity**point**: **Your value does not come from what you look like, what you experience, or what you do.** It comes from your love and the fact that you are a divine, irreplaceable child of God.

You do not have to be perfect *(or anything close to it)* to have infinite, absolute value, but you might have a subconscious policy that disagrees. The Voice of Fear might say you have to be perfect to have any value at all. You might be driving yourself crazy trying to do everything *perfectly* to earn love and validation. You might spend half the night thinking about all the things you need to do or get to feel better about yourself. I have had a subconscious policy that said, "You have to do everything perfectly or you won't be loved."

Do you have that one? Are you trying to earn lots of money, keep a perfect house, have a perfect body, raise perfect kids, or be a perfect Christian? Are you chasing plaques on the wall, clothes, recognition, or a certain amount of money that will finally make you feel successful? *These things are never going to do it.* Getting new things or achieving recognition might make you and your ego feel good temporarily, but the satisfaction will be quickly replaced by the need for other things you still don't have. Most people think that once they lose the weight or make more money they will finally feel good about themselves, but they are usually disappointed when they get there to find that they don't feel better.

This happens because real self-worth can't be earned. Real self-worth comes from understanding the truth about who you are and understanding that your value is infinite and absolute no matter what. This is the only way to peace.

No matter what you do or what you get, your Voice of Fear will still tell you that you aren't good enough anyway. It *always* tells you that you need something more to prove your value. If you keep trying to create peace by getting things, you will always lose. *The only way to win this game is not to play.* Stop thinking of yourself in terms of performance and assets; they are not who you are. *Your love is who you are.*

There is another subconscious thought process that might be influencing how you value yourself, and it involves fear of what other people think of you. At this very moment you are probably basing your value on how other people value you, even though most of the time you don't even know what these people really think. You are assuming what they think based on behavior you interpreted. In truth, most people don't think about you at all. They are too focused on their own stuff. And if they do think about you, they probably don't think what you think they think. You are most likely projecting your own fears of not being good enough onto them. *What you think they think tells you more about your own opinion of yourself than theirs.*

I spent three years quite convinced my next door neighbor didn't like us. I interpreted some of his behavior to mean he didn't like being neighbors with us. Our yard is a little out of control and I was afraid he didn't like our weeds. For three years I steered clear of him and wasn't very friendly because I thought he didn't like us. Then one day we happened to be out working in our yards and he came over to speak to me. He was kind and friendly, and during the course of our conversation I realized he had never had any ill feelings towards us at all. My fear of not being good enough had created the whole thing.

Your Voice of Fear skews the way you see people and situations and applies your fear that you might not be good enough to every situation, even where it doesn't belong. I had projected my fear of not being good enough onto my neighbor and thought he didn't like us. Living in my fear had made me selfish and unloving towards him. I let the fear of what he thought of me change the way I behaved.

The moral of this story is *you can stop worrying about what other people think of you because it's irrelevant.* You are the same you, no matter what they think. Remember that most of the people you allow to judge you have fears skewing their perspectives, too, so they aren't accurate judges of anything. Besides, their opinions don't change who you are. You are the same you no matter what they think.

clarity**point**: **You cannot be diminished by what other people think of you.** Your value is infinite and absolute. It does not change. What other people think of you is irrelevant.

Nothing anyone says or thinks about you can hurt you or diminish you in any way, unless you let it. Others can think you are heartless, mean, ugly, horrible, stupid, or whatever. It doesn't change anything. You are still the same you and your value is still the same.

But no one can save you from yourself. You can choose to focus on your faults and mistakes and live in fear that you're not good enough if you want to. If you choose to feel inferior and let past situations and bad choices define you, that is your choice. But no one can make you feel inferior or diminish you without your permission, and no one can make you feel valued without your permission either. You get to decide how you will esteem yourself, but if you don't consciously choose to value yourself correctly (for your infinite and absolute value), your subconscious mind will automatically choose an inaccurate, fear-based policy that will leave you feeling worthless. *(Read that again and make sure you get it.)*

This is a battle you will have to fight every moment of every day, because the Voice of Fear in your head will always tell you that you aren't good enough. Every moment you are alive, it will try to distract and discourage you with fear-based thoughts about your value. It will also encourage behavior that is inaccurate, immature, and emotional. It wants you to behave like a drama queen, a jerk, a victim, or a control freak, and if you listen, your behavior will be way beneath who you are – *a divine, irreplaceable, amazing soul.*

So don't listen to it. Take the time to write some personal policies about how you are going to value yourself from this day forward and how you are going to deal with what other people think of you. You can use my personal policies about this as examples:

My Personal Policies about My Value

This is my policy for determining my own value:

I am an amazing, irreplaceable, infinitely valuable child of God. My value comes from that fact alone.

My value is absolute. This means nothing I do, nothing anyone thinks about me, and no situation, mistake, or experience can change it. My value is not affected by what I look like, how much money I make, or what I do. My value was set by God and does not change. Mistakes I make and difficult situations I experience are just locations on my journey. They are just lessons, and they do not affect my value.

I officially give myself permission to be a work in progress. I do not have to be perfect to have absolute value. I am a student in the classroom of life and I am right on track in my personal process of becoming.

I own the responsibility for determining my own value. I do not expect anyone else to make me feel valued and important. That must come from inside me. Once I know my value is set and absolute, I can accept love and validation from others, and believe it.

This is my policy about what other people think of me:

What other people think of me is irrelevant. I am the same me no matter what they think. This is my official policy. I care about other people, but I don't care what they think of me. I know who I am and I do not give that power away to anyone else.

This is my policy about my past mistakes:

My value is infinite and absolute, so my mistakes, flaws, and failures do not affect it. They are things I am working to overcome because I want to become the best possible me, but they are a perfect part of who I am at this place in my journey. They do not take away from my value. I have a strict policy against comparing myself to other people — it is against my rules to do so. If the Voice of Fear in my head starts comparing, I quickly remind myself that that is against my rules.

My self-esteem is my responsibly. No one can give it to me and no one can take it away. I am the one in charge of how I feel about me. I choose to see my goodness and focus on my love.

Are you feeling inspired? Turn to your notebook and create your new policies now.

8 – A Safety Net

In the last chapter you worked on some policies about trusting your true value. In this chapter you have the chance to create some personal policies about trusting the process of life so you can experience joy and peace even when the journey is rough.

I know firsthand how difficult and scary the classroom of life can be. My journey has been wrought with problems, disappointments, and challenges. Many of these challenging classes I signed up for with bad choices I made, but sometimes it feels like the universe signs us up for classes, like it or not. Some of these required classes are extremely painful and we often struggle to find balance and the strength to keep going. Life can sometimes feel like a terrifying walk across a tightrope.

As a child I remember going to the circus and watching a man riding a bicycle across a wire. The people around me were on the edges of their seats, scared to death every time he wobbled and almost fell. Personally I wasn't impressed with the act. I could plainly see that the performer was in no danger. There was a giant net underneath him the entire time that guaranteed his safety. Even at a young age I could see that having a net took the fear out of the journey.

Does your life feel like a white-knuckle walk across a tightrope? Does life feel like a balancing act wrought with danger because you could fail, fall, or die in the process? Do you feel at risk every step of the way?

Many people walk through life scared to death about all the bad things that could happen to them, but they and YOU don't have to feel this way. You could choose to believe and trust there's a net. You could choose to believe you are safely in God's hands the entire time. You could choose to believe that the universe was created to serve you, and because of this you are never at risk here. You could choose to believe that your value is absolute because your journey is a classroom, not a test. These principles could be your net.

If you choose to believe there is a net, life will still be a tricky balancing act; it will still be challenging. But it will not be the white-knuckle experience you are used to because you will know you aren't really in danger. You are safe the whole time.

The problem is that you can't see the net and it is difficult to trust something you can't see. On top of that, life looks and feels dangerous! There are painful experiences and opportunities to fail all around you, and bad things happen to good people all the time. Some people think that trusting in some invisible net, in spite of obvious danger all around us, amounts to nothing but optimistic denial. Some people think I have my head in the clouds because I choose to believe in a net I can't see or prove. But trusting the process of life, believing in a net, and feeling safe would be a good idea even if there weren't a net, because the only other option is to walk the wire in fear and suffering, which would make your required classes even worse.

Either way you have to walk the wire, and you are going to experience lots of difficulties and challenges throughout your life. I think you might as well do it feeling safe and loved.

I also really believe there is a net because I don't believe a loving God (or a loving force in the universe) would send me (or you) here without one. *Would you let your child walk a tightrope without a net?*

I also believe the universe was created for our education, not for our destruction. We are here to learn to love, not to be weeded out or lost. Life is a classroom, and it can be a really difficult classroom, but it is not a test. Your life will always be the perfect classroom journey for you, and every experience that shows up on your journey is here to serve you. There is meaning and purpose behind everything that happens. There are no accidents, which means your suffering through difficulties is never for nothing. Your life matters and everything you experience matters. Your trials are here to help you become a better person, and trusting this is truth will take some of the sting out of them. *Suffering becomes more bearable if it at least counts for something.*

I learned this principle from Dr. Frankl, who said, "I am convinced that, in the final analysis, there is no situation that does not contain within it the seed of meaning." He said this might be an overly optimistic view of life, but he believed "there are no tragic, negative aspects [of life] which could not be, by the stand one takes to them, transmuted into positive accomplishments."

Dr. Frankl taught that an optimistic view of life – seeing meaning and purpose in everything that happens – can get you through the painful parts of your journey a little easier. I agree. This might be an overly optimistic attitude, but it is a good choice if it makes your journey less painful.

Clients often ask me why a loving God doesn't just show us the net, because that would really help; we could just know there is nothing to fear. I think it would make the journey too easy. An invisible net provides you with the opportunity to learn trust. If you had all the answers and could see the net, it would require no stretching on your part. But you don't need to see it to know it's there.

Think about this logically. *God is love.* He loves you. Seeing you smashed into a hundred pieces isn't His objective for your life. Losing you is not part of His plan. His objective is not to weed his children out. His objective is for us to learn. When we make mistakes it just means more learning is needed. God wants to help us learn the lesson and get back on the wire and try again. This journey and this universe (and everything God created) are here to serve your safe, yet exciting, process of learning. There is nothing to fear.

Life is not out to get you even though it feels that way sometimes. You are totally safe every step of the way. *(At least you have the option of seeing life that way if you want to.)* Life is about learning to walk the tightrope, find your balance, and trust God, life, and yourself in the process. And you can do this because there is really nothing to fear. *When you get this concept, it will change everything.*

The two core fears that scare you most, and have created most of the suffering in your life, are actually not even possible. You are afraid of things that aren't even real. You are afraid you aren't good enough, when your value is infinite and absolute and not on the line. You are afraid of loss and not getting the life you wanted, when your journey is always the perfect classroom journey for you. In reality *there is no failure and there is no loss* (except the losses you are meant to experience so that you can grow).

You will experience much more happiness in life if you choose to accept these truths and see your journey as a safe one. Choose to trust the process of life and believe that even if you fall, fail, struggle, suffer, and even die, *you are still okay.*

This concept can take a little pondering to get, but it is absolutely true. There is meaning and purpose behind every experience you have, and no matter the depth, scope, or length of your life, it will always serve your perfect process of growth.

This is probably the most important lesson I learned from studying the work of Dr. Frankl and others who have survived great suffering. Every experience you have, no matter how difficult or hopeless it seems, is in your life to serve you in some way. Your suffering is never for naught.

Throughout my life I have watched people battle enormous fear when terrible things happened to them. In the end, most of them decide to trust that the experience was meant to happen. They decide to believe that this is how things are supposed to be because this mindset makes them feel more peaceful and positive.

Whenever I teach this concept to a group, though, someone inevitably points out that I cannot prove that there is meaning and purpose in everything and that life is always your perfect classroom. They are right of course. I cannot prove that life will always be the perfect journey for you. I cannot prove there are no accidents and everything happens for a reason. I cannot prove there is a net and that you are safe every step of the way. I cannot prove that any of this is truth... *but you can't prove that it's not truth.*

That being the case, you get to choose how you want to experience your life. Would you like to live in fear, or in trust and love? The universe will never force a mindset on you. You have complete free agency to choose fear and suffer unnecessarily if you want to. If you would like to live each day with anxiety and stress, you can. Remember that fear is your autopilot setting because of your subconscious policies. So if you don't consciously choose trust, safety, and love, your subconscious mind will choose fear.

To make this battle easier, I'm going to teach you exactly how to consciously choose trust and make your fears disappear so you can experience more peace and success. This concept is one of the most important things you will learn in this book.

The first step on the path to fearlessness is to embrace two critical principles of truth that are the opposites of the two core fears (the fear of failure and the fear of loss). If you practice trusting these two truths you can eliminate fear in any situation.

The first is to trust that your value isn't on the line because life is a classroom, not a test.

The second is to trust that your journey is the perfect classroom journey for you; that anything you lose, you are meant to lose; and that each experience serves you no matter what happens.

Trusting in your value and your journey will take the fear out of any situation. But you have to practice trusting these two truths. Your trusting muscle may be very out of shape (it may be a muscle you have never used), and it's going to take some work to get that muscle in shape. Many of my clients say it feels almost impossible at first to choose trust in their value and their journey, but after working on it for a while it gets easier, and they start to see they have the power to change the way they feel in any moment – they can choose their way out of fear.

clarity**point**: **Choose to trust these two critical truths that are the opposites of the two core fears:**

> 1) Your value is infinite and absolute because life is a classroom.
>
> 2) Every experience is your perfect classroom journey.

Take some time to write a new personal policy about trusting the process of life and believing there's a net. If you make this your official policy and read it often, it will change the way you feel about everything in your life. Trusting your journey brings amazing Clarity like you have never experienced before. It takes the stress out of every situation and gives you confidence and peace.

This is one of the most important policies you will create, so take some time and get it right. Remember to read through all your policies on a daily basis to internalize them.

My Personal Policy about Trusting the Process of Life

It is my official policy that there is a net. I know my journey here is a safe one and I have nothing to fear. I trust the net and believe I am safely in God's hands all the time.

My two core fears are the fear of not being good enough and the fear of loss. To battle these two fears I choose to trust that my value isn't on the line and I choose to see my life as the perfect classroom journey for me. Every experience I have serves my process of growth. When things go wrong and I experience loss or disappointment, I remind myself that even though I can't see the reason behind the experience yet, it is in my life to bless and serve me. And God will use this experience to help me become my highest, best self. There is meaning and purpose in everything.

Because I trust God and life, I can also trust myself. I understand that mistakes I make don't affect my value and that each teaches me something valuable. I can easily erase these mistakes and try again.

I also trust that my inner truth has all the answers I need, every step of the way. I always listen to my gut feelings and trust them. The more I do this, the more I know that I'm right on track and where I'm supposed to be.

Every minute of every day I choose to see the net and walk forward, trusting God, life, and myself.

Create your new policies in your notebook now.

9 – Trusting Life

Carol was clearly miserable, and she was feeling a great deal of resentment towards her husband because he was not able to make enough money to support their family. College had not been an option for him, so he had done the best he could to find a career and had secured a job in construction. He worked hard, but he didn't bring home enough money to support their large family.

This meant that Carol had to work too. She was very successful in her career and made good money, but it required long hours and was very stressful. She felt a lot of pressure as she tried to balance being a mom, caring for a family, and earning a living. This pressure created all kinds of fear-based thoughts and feelings. Carol was very jealous of her friends whose husbands made more money and whose lives seemed easier. This jealousy created resentment towards her husband and was causing problems in their marriage.

As I got to know Carol better, I was extremely impressed with the work she was doing and the person she was becoming. She was a smart businesswoman and was accomplishing amazing things in her community. I was impressed by the personal growth she had experienced and how her work was changing her as a person.

One day in coaching I asked Carol, "What would you do differently if your husband had a successful career and could provide for your family without your income?"

Her answer was simple: "I would stay home and not work, I would enjoy more leisure activities, and life would be easier and more fun."

"Well," I said, "it's a good thing that didn't happen then! The world would have missed out on a talented, compassionate, brilliant woman and the gifts she is giving."

If she could have, Carol would have taken the easy way out. She would not have stretched, grown, or contributed to the world the way she had. She might have had more fun if she hadn't had to work, but she would not have become the woman she was becoming. She would not have done the good she was doing. She would not have done it if she hadn't had to. She would have stayed home and done less, and she would have become less.

I asked her if she was open to the possibility that the universe sent this husband to her because he was the perfect husband for her. Because he didn't earn enough income for the family, he provided the perfect opportunity for her to grow, learn, and become all she was meant to be. What if the universe knew she wouldn't work if she didn't have to, so it didn't give her that option?

She immediately realized that was truth. Her life was exactly as it was meant to be. She was becoming the woman she was meant to be and doing the things the world needed her to do. Everything happens for a reason.

You, too, can choose to see your journey as perfect even when it isn't fun. You can choose to trust that there is meaning and purpose behind everything that happens to you. You can accept the fact that your life will rarely turn out the way you expect it to or want it to, yet it will always turn out in a way that best serves your process of becoming. Trusting in this means not getting so bent out of shape when your life surprises you. It means choosing to believe that there is a reason things happen, even when you can't see the reason. It means choosing an attitude of trust and love instead of letting your Voice of Fear drive you to feel impatient, bitter, or angry. Real happiness is only possible when you choose to experience trust and gratitude for your life exactly as it is right now.

* *

clarity**point**: **Life is supposed to surprise you. If it were predictable and smooth, you wouldn't learn anything.** This classroom experience almost never turns out the way you expect, but it is always the right life for you.

* *

It will bring great peace to your life if you stop judging every experience as good or bad. Don't be so quick to see situations as negative when you can't yet see the outcome. Often bad situations lead you to something better than you had before. Sometimes good things end up being big disappointments. *You never know what you're going to get.* Every day is a grand adventure into the great unknown, and you cannot know what lies around the next corner. So with the unknown before you, you have only two choices: you can live in trust (believing you are safe and that good things are coming) or you can live in fear (scared of the future and focused on you). *Your choice will not change what's around that next corner; it will be what it's meant to be, but it will have a big impact on the way you feel today.* Do you want to experience today in fear, focused on yourself? Or do you want to experience trust, and focus on love? It's up to you.

. . . .

clarity**point**: **Happiness does not come from getting what you want; it comes from trusting what you get.**

. . . .

This is the cold, hard truth: Life rarely meets your expectations. You will almost never perform as well as you want to, events will usually not turn out as you planned them, and people will usually disappoint you. *Get used to it.*

With this more realistic perspective, you can now decide how you want to experience each of these situations. It's your life and it's your choice. You can live this day in gratitude and trust, or you can suffer.

Jonah's Story

Jonah was frustrated because he hadn't achieved the financial success he expected to have at that point in his life. He had big plans for his career, but felt like a failure because they had not worked out. This expectation was seriously affecting his self-esteem.

The crazy part was that Jonah was only a failure measured against the standards and policies he had created. He had made the rules. He was the one who had decided he should be at a certain level by a certain age to be good enough. No one else thought his value depended on reaching that goal. His family and friends thought he was doing great. (His misery was self-inflicted. Is yours?)

Jonah realized he needed to change his policy regarding success. He also needed to trust the process of life and let go of his desire to control it. Though his career had not gone the way he wanted, the path it had taken had provided many interesting opportunities to learn. He decided it made more sense to trust that he was on track in his perfect journey. He made a policy to ignore everything his Voice of Fear said that made him feel bad, and choose gratitude instead.

If you create a lot of expectations about life, yourself, your performance, and other people, and if you do this on a regular basis, you are most likely miserable, disappointed, discouraged, and frustrated a great deal of the time. *You don't have to live this way.*

You can change the way you experience every disappointing or frustrating situation by asking yourself the following questions:

1. What is this experience here to show me about myself?

2. What is it here to teach me?

3. How is it giving me an opportunity to grow or to learn to love at a higher level?

Write down the answers that come to you. This process helps you get into trust about your journey. It would serve you immensely if you were to write a personal policy about how you are going to handle disappointments. You might want to make the questions above your official procedure. If you don't have a procedure outlined ahead of time, your subconscious programming will take over and you might handle these situations poorly. How are you going to respond when things don't work out the way you wanted them to? Here is an example of my personal policy:

My Personal Policy about Disappointment

I trust the process of my life even when I get disappointed or frustrated with a situation. I know that things happen for a reason and that there are no accidents. My life is the perfect classroom journey for me. In every situation I ask myself:

1. *What is this experience here to show me about myself?*

2. *What is it here to teach me?*

3. *How is it giving me an opportunity to grow?*

If I can see the lesson, it helps me trust and be grateful for the experience as it is. It is my official policy to trust God no matter what happens.

I believe that everything that happens serves me and my process of learning in some way. When I choose to see everything as perfect and serving me, I get bent out of shape less and experience more peace.

This is how I choose to live.

Turn to your notebook and write a new personal policy about trusting your journey when things go wrong.

10 – Love Is the Answer

Because I write a weekly advice column, people often ask me for advice. Most of the time, regardless of the specifics of their situation, love is my answer. You usually can't go wrong if you choose love.

The problem is that when you are suffering from *a fear of failure or a fear of loss,* you are not capable of love. You must first choose trust in your value and your journey so that you are no longer needy and scared. It is only when you need nothing that you can show up for others and not have strings attached. When you are scared, your neediness automatically makes your acts of kindness about getting what you need. You may still do loving, kind things for people, but you will be doing them partly for you. You will be doing them to get the validation or approval you need to quiet your fear, and that isn't really love.

Every time I explain this to a group someone asks me, "Isn't it still a good thing to serve and love people even if you are trying to validate your own worth in the process?" Yes it is, but you might not get the appreciation you are hoping for. The problem with loving behavior when you are acting from fear is that others can feel it. They know your generosity isn't really about them, and they often see you as phony, resent you, and don't appreciate what you did for them. They can subconsciously feel that it was more about you.

If you are one of those people who serve and give too much – who have made self-sacrifice your mission in life – you may find that people don't appreciate you and even take your service for granted. They might even feel entitled to your sacrifices. You might find yourself starting to resent them, and this might cause serious riffs in your relationships. Too much self-sacrifice doesn't serve anyone in the end because it is fear-driven. You must make sure you are taking care of yourself *and* serving others at the same time, not just one or the other. You must have balance.

Real love can only happen when you are in trust about your infinite and absolute value and your journey so you know you're safe. Real love can only happen when you don't need anything from the other person because your bucket is already full. In this place, with nothing to fear, you are not only capable of love, but you will subconsciously, automatically want to give more attention and validation to others. Without fear in the mix, you can be the real you.

clarity**point**: **When you are in trust about your value, you are capable of love towards others.**

When you choose trust about your value and your journey, you will also be able to see other people accurately, as the same as you. You will see their infinite value as the same as yours. You will see that though we all have different talents, gifts, personalities, strengths, and weaknesses, we are signed up for different classes, so our journeys are vastly different. But no person is any better or any worse than anyone else; we all have the same value. You must see every person who crosses your path as an amazing, divine, scared, struggling human being, in process just like you.

* *

clarity**point**:   **When you experience the Clarity that comes when you choose trust and love, you can see other people accurately – as the same as you.**

* *

The Voice of Fear in your head doesn't see people accurately, though. It always sees them as better than you or worse than you. It spends a great deal of time casting anyone who is different from you as the bad guy so you can feel like the good guy. This tendency to see other people as different from you is a deeply ingrained human behavior. It is also the root cause of all the conflict, fighting, wars, prejudice, hate, and drama on this planet, and is responsible for most of the fighting in your home and the drama in your office. This mentality causes jealousy and an unhealthy level of competition to prove who is better. It causes judgment, criticism, and gossip, and we all do it. We just can't stop seeing ourselves as different from or better than other people.

Think about whom you tend to judge. Do you see yourself as better than them? Can you see how you might be casting them as bad guys to see yourself as the good guy? If there is any group of people that is different from you in any way (by culture, race, sexual orientation, social status, etc.) or that you don't understand, you might be inaccurately casting them as bad guys.

At other times your Voice of Fear might see other people as better than you. When this happens you might experience some self-pity drama about how inadequate you are, though even in this situation you might subconsciously look for something bad in them so you can turn it around and see them as worse than you in the end.

Another tendency to watch out for is letting your Voice of Fear convince you that the other person was bad first even though you both behaved badly. You might actually think that because they were bad first you were justified in being bad back. You therefore are the good guy and they are the bad one. The problem is that being bad back is just as bad as being bad first.

At the end of this chapter you will have a chance to write a new official policy about seeing people as the same as you. Changing the way you have been seeing people your whole life might feel difficult at first. Your subconscious mind will really want to hold on to your old pattern of seeing others as better or worse. *But your conscious mind is more powerful than your subconscious mind. You have the power to override your old subconscious policies.* You just have to consciously decide to see people accurately.

· ·

clarity**point**: **Your conscious mind is more powerful than your subconscious mind.** You have the power to override your subconscious policies in any moment and consciously choose truth, trust, and love.

· ·

The good news is you have the capacity to do this because the real you (love) knows the truth – that we are all amazing, divine, struggling, scared human beings doing the best we can with what we know at the time; that everyone's value is infinite and absolute; that we are all students in the classroom of life, fighting a battle with fear, and that our fear sometimes encourages some really bad behavior; that we all give in to this fear and behave badly on occasion, and that we all do it because we are all the same.

By the way, seeing others as the same as you does not mean you agree with them or condone their behavior. It doesn't mean you have to be friends with them. It just means you see their value as the same as yours – *infinite and absolute.* It also means you will set aside your fear towards them, forgive them, give them permission to be a work in progress, and admit that you're not perfect either. We are all the same. We are all fighting this battle with fear and inaccuracy, and we are all afraid we aren't good enough.

clarity**point**: **Everyone on this planet experiences fear that they aren't good enough, and this fear produces some really bad, selfish behavior.**

Most people spend the majority of their lives in fear, focused on themselves, casting everyone around them as bad guys. They almost can't help it because it happens subconsciously and they don't know any other way to be. When you understand that most human behavior is driven by fear, you will understand why people hurt or offend you. You will understand it isn't about you at all. *Their bad behavior is caused by their fear of failure and loss.* It is not about you. It is usually about their need for validation, approval, or security. When you understand this you also understand that all bad behavior is really a request for love, attention, or validation. Bad behavior doesn't make you want to love them, but it is what they need.

clarity**point**: **Fear is the root cause of most bad behavior.** When others behave badly, it is not about you; it is about their fear of not being good enough or their fear of loss.

clarity**point**: **All bad behavior is really a request for love, attention, or validation.**

When people experience fear of failure or loss, they behave badly and often create stories that cast you as the bad guy. They do this so they can feel better about themselves. *But remember, it's just a story, and just because they believe this story doesn't make it true.* Their Voice of Fear created the story because they can't accurately see their own value and they need to put other people down to feel safe. Don't take this kind of bad behavior personally – it's not about you. It's about their fear. Besides, what other people think of you is irrelevant because your value is absolute and can't be diminished. If you can't be hurt you can let most offenses roll off.

Don't let their fear (and bad behavior) trigger your fear and make you behave badly. Remember that your value isn't on the line, and you are bulletproof. Stay in trust and love no matter what they do or say. If you can do this, they will be forced to take responsibility for their bad behavior. If you behave badly back, they will not take responsibility for their bad behavior because they will be too focused on yours. (Read that again.)

. . . .

clarity**point**: **Love is the right way to handle every situation.** Sometimes this means giving service or validation to another person and sometimes it means taking care of you. Either way, act in love, not fear.

. . . .

You must also avoid seeing other people as better than you. This is another common subconscious program. You might even think it is righteous to see other people as better than you. You might think that humility requires self-deprecation or self-sacrifice. You might even let other people walk on you or take advantage of you in order to feel like a nice person. You might think of this as *"being too nice,"* but this overly nice behavior is based in fear, not love. You are sacrificing yourself too much because you are afraid you aren't good enough, and you are trying to get love and validation from other people to quiet that fear. The Voice of Fear is behind this overly selfless, victim-mentality, co-dependent, doormat behavior, and *it is unworthy of the amazing, important being you really are.*

Real love is an appropriate awareness and accurate valuing of yourself and other people. When there is no fear skewing your perspective, you can clearly see, in each moment, when it is appropriate to sacrifice and give to other people because you love them, and when it is appropriate to take care of yourself because you love you, too. In each situation your Voice of Truth will tell you which is appropriate so you can maintain balance.

You can be out of balance the other way, too, though, and become too selfish. You might get sick of being a doormat and decide not to let people walk on you anymore. You might become distrustful, defensive and feel a need to protect yourself from other people. You might see people as threats and focus your energy on protecting you. When you behave this way you might think you are coming across as strong, but your fear shows through. Defensiveness can actually make you look weak, because it is a subconscious announcement that you see yourself as diminishable. If you saw yourself as infinite and absolute, you would need no defense. People with real confidence and strength don't get offended or defensive very often. They need no defense because they cannot be hurt.

Real strength comes from the absence of fear. Real strength comes from living in trust and love and knowing that nothing can diminish you. In this place you can say no, defend yourself, and speak your truth about anything and do it in a loving way. You can be *strong and loving* at the same time.

You can start living this way today. You just have to write a personal policy about love and seeing human behavior accurately. You might also need a procedure to help you put this policy to work in your life. Here is one suggestion: Every time someone behaves badly towards you and you aren't sure how to respond, sit down with a piece of paper and answer the following questions:

1. Write down what this person did to you.

2. Ask yourself what they are afraid of that might be behind their behavior.

3. Are they casting you as the bad guy?

4. Are you casting them as the bad guy?

5. Could you choose to see them as the same as you?

6. What you are afraid of that could influence your reaction?

7. What do you really want to have happen? What would be the best possible outcome?

8. What could you do to create that outcome?

Once you are clear about what you want and are seeing the person accurately, write down your options for responding (think of as many as you can). You could respond with anger and lash out to defend yourself. You could respond by ignoring the situation and hoping it goes away on its own. You could forgive this person for being imperfect and let it go. You could choose to have a mutually validating conversation and really listen to the other person before asking permission to share your feelings.

Once you have written down as many options as you can think of, see if you can tell which ones are fear-based and which ones are love-based. (Hint: The fear-based ones are focused on you and making you feel better, and they probably don't honor the other person.) Cross out all the fear-based options and pick a love-based option that feels right to you and honors the intrinsic value in both of you. Your Voice of Truth will guide you to the right response. There is a free Clarity Questions Worksheet on my website you can use to step you through this process.

You will also want to take the time to write some policies about seeing people and situations accurately. Here are my personal policy and procedure to get you started:

My Personal Policy and Procedure about Love and Seeing People Accurately

This is my policy about seeing other people and their behavior accurately:

> *The Voice of Fear in my head has a tendency to see other people as either better than me or worse than me. It instantly casts them into the roles of good guys or bad guys. When I see people this way I am not seeing them accurately. I choose to override this tendency by consciously seeing everyone as the same as me. We are all connected, we are all God's children, and we all have the same value. We are all struggling, scared, divine, amazing, eternal beings in a process of learning and growing. We have different gifts and talents, and we are signed up for different classes down here, but our value is the same.*
>
> *I commit to seeing people accurately with love and wisdom.*

This is my procedure for when people behave badly:

> *When people behave badly it is my policy to step back from their bad behavior and look for fear. I ask myself, "What are they afraid of?" When people behave badly it is usually not about me; it is usually about their fears about themselves. This means most bad behavior is really a request for love, attention, or validation.*

Some people allow me to love them, but some are too scared to accept it. Either way I see them accurately and choose love.

If I respond with love, it helps them see and own their bad behavior. I choose love because that is the kind of person I want to be.

Go to your notebook now and create your policies about seeing other people accurately and how to respond when they behave badly.

11 – The Clarity Formula

$his is the most important chapter* in *Choosing Clarity* because I will teach you exactly how to choose trust and love in every moment of your life and thereby escape fear. I will teach you a clearly defined yet very simple procedure to help you do this. I call this procedure The Clarity Formula™, and if you will practice it, running through the steps in your mind numerous times a day, you will experience fearlessness.

Think about what your life might feel like without fear. What if you could approach every situation trusting that you are safe and knowing that nothing can hurt or diminish you? What if you could live each day knowing your value was infinite and absolute, and seeing every experience as a lesson?

I really want you to experience your life this way. I believe God and the universe want you to experience your life this way, too. So whenever you find yourself experiencing fear, just run through the four simple formula steps in your mind. It works because fear cannot exist where there is trust and love. Darkness and light cannot exist at the same time in the same place. To eliminate the darkness from your life, all you have to do is consciously choose light in every moment.

. . . .

claritypoint: **You cannot experience trust and love and fear at the same time.** When you choose trust and love, all fear disappears.

. . . .

Think of a situation that triggers your fear of failure or loss, then run through the formula steps one by one and see how it might change how you feel in that situation.

The Clarity Formula™

When I experience fear, I can consciously choose a state of trust and love by choosing these four things:

I choose to trust that…

1. My value is not on the line because life is a classroom, not a test. My value is infinite and absolute. I'm good enough right now.

2. My life is the perfect classroom journey for me. There are no accidents and every experience is a lesson that serves me in some way.

I also choose love. I choose…

1. To see the other person or people involved in this situation as the same as me.

2. To be a giver (instead of a getter) of love and validation in this moment. I choose love for myself and for others at the same time.

This simple formula can completely change how you experience your life. If you will practice choosing trust in your value and in your journey, and if you will choose to see people accurately, as the same as you, and to love them, *you will discover a peace and happiness you cannot even imagine.* But if you don't consciously choose to go through these steps and choose trust and love in any specific moment, your subconscious mind will choose for you and it will choose fear. *(Are you getting that point from the repetition?)*

clarity**point**:   **If you don't consciously choose trust and love, your subconscious mind will choose for you, and it usually chooses fear.**

Amy's Story

Amy came to me for coaching because she was worried about giving an upcoming speech. The last time she had given a speech in public she had experienced embarrassing stage fright, and she didn't want that to happen again. We spent some time working on her policies about the purpose and nature of life. Changing her perspective on these two things helped her see the speech as a learning opportunity in which her value wasn't on the line. Next I taught her the Clarity Formula and she practiced it at home for a few weeks before the big speech.

Amy found herself repeating over and over throughout every day "trust and love," "trust and love," "trust and love." This mantra replaced the thoughts and feelings of fear and stress she usually experienced. She found herself more focused on other people, too. She was able to control her thinking and be a lot more caring.

On the day of the big speech she felt remarkably calm. Because she had been practicing the formula, she was generally less scared of anything. But right before she went on stage she ran through the steps again. She reminded herself that her value was not on the line. No matter how the speech turned out, her value was the same. She also decided to trust the process of life and believe that the speech would turn out perfectly no matter how it went.

She was now capable of love because her fear of failure and her fear of loss were off the table. Next she decided to remember that everyone in the room understood her nervousness because they battled the fear of loss and failure, too. She remembered that we are all the same and that no one is better than anyone else. Then she chose love. She decided to focus on serving the people in the room, and that the speech was really not about her; it was about delivering a message these people needed to hear. She chose to focus on serving, showing up for them, and giving to them instead of worrying about herself and how she looked. This last step totally took away her fear. When you focus on love, fear disappears.

If you want things to change in your life or business, take control of your thinking and start consciously choosing how you want to experience each situation. Choosing trust and love is easier, though, if you have clearly defined policies and procedures in place ahead of time.

Take some time to write down your personal policies and procedures for using the Clarity Formula and consciously choosing your mindset in every situation.

My Personal Policy and Procedure about Choosing Trust and Love

This is my policy for choosing trust and love:

> *I have the power to choose how I want to experience each moment of my life. There are only two choices: fear or Clarity. I choose to live my life in Clarity. I do this by consciously choosing trust and love in each situation.*
>
> *I use the Clarity Formula to help me do this.*

This is my procedure for choosing trust and love:

> *In every situation I review the Clarity Formula in my mind. I consciously choose to trust that my value isn't on the line. I have nothing to fear because I am good enough right now. My value is infinite and absolute and nothing that happens can change that. I also choose to trust that my life is the perfect classroom journey for me. Every experience that shows up in my life is here for a reason, and that reason is my growth and learning.*

In every situation I choose to see the other people involved as the same as me. We are all struggling, scared, divine, amazing human beings in process. I give others permission to be students in the classroom of life, just like me.

I am not intimidated by other people and I never talk down to anyone. I see everyone as the same as me.

I choose to live by and be my love. Everywhere I go I look for opportunities to lift and edify other people (validate their worth by giving them honor, respect, and encouragement). I am a giver, not a getter. I look for people who need some encouragement or a kind hello. I am here to be an expression of God's love — it is who I am. I let others feel God's love for them through me. This is my official procedure in each situation.

Go to your notebook and create your new personal policies and procedures for choosing trust and love.

12 – The Chick and the Egg

It is fairly easy to choose trust and love when things are going well in your life, but it gets extremely difficult when your life falls apart *(which it will on occasion)*. It can even stay fallen apart for long periods of time, and you can start to doubt that anyone cares. You might start to feel that life is against you instead of a perfect process to serve you. You might start to doubt the net, God, and yourself.

Have you ever felt this way? Are you discouraged that life isn't turning out the way you wanted it to? Do you feel unimportant or unloved? Are you frustrated that God isn't doing more to help you? If you feel this way, let me help you look at this situation from a fresh perspective.

When a baby chick hatches, it often struggles for a long, long time, and you can get impatient watching the little guy struggle. You might be tempted to help him out and break a little bit of the shell away and make it easier for him to escape, but if you do, *he will die.* You will rob him of a process specifically designed to make him strong. It is only through this struggle that he can gain the strength to survive his life.

It is crucial *(if you love him)* that you let him struggle his way out of this challenge on his own.

Your life works the same way. The challenges you currently face are there to help you become stronger and smarter, too. They are probably forcing you to learn and grow. If you were rescued from this situation, it might rob you of a process you need to become the person you are meant to be.

. . . .

clarity**point**: **You are meant to be more than you currently are.** The universe knows this. It is bringing you the perfect challenges you need to become your best.

. . . .

The universe uses every experience you have to help you grow and learn. No experience is wasted. Every choice you make and everything that happens to you because of other people's choices become your perfect lessons. As you learn to trust this truth, you will experience less fear and more peace.

But the Voice of Fear in your head doesn't want you to experience peace. It wants you to get discouraged, upset, and angry about your challenges. It wants you to dwell in frustration and disappointment that your life isn't easier. It uses your struggles against you to stop you from learning and make you doubt your Voice of Truth.

It does this by using the difficult experiences in your life to make you doubt your value and your journey. It tells you these problems are in your life because you aren't good enough. It tells you God doesn't care about you, your life doesn't matter, and He will probably reject you in the end. It tells you that your life is a mess or ruined and is beyond repair.

Don't listen to it. Your Voice of Fear does this because it wants to distract you from learning and loving. Don't let this happen. Wake up and consciously recognize what is happening in your head and that *your Voice of Fear is driving these thoughts.* Most of what it says is not even true, so you must trust the process of your life even when things go wrong and you start to feel hopeless.

If you practice doing this, you will experience more peace. You will find meaning, purpose, and even achievement in the very worst of situations. *You will see that there are no circumstances, however negative, that don't serve you on some level.* If you choose to see your experiences as lessons that serve your process of growth, you can literally turn tragedies into accomplishments just like Dr. Frankl said you can.

Conrad's Story

Conrad was really discouraged with life and about at the end of his rope when he came to me for coaching. The bills were piling up and nothing he tried to solve his financial problems was working. He was praying (begging might be a better word) for help or a way out, and he was starting to feel abandoned because help wasn't coming.

We clarified his policy about the purpose of life, which is to learn and love other people. Then we talked about why help might not be coming, and he decided this situation was probably in his life to help him grow and learn. He could see that fighting his way out of these problems, working hard, and creating solutions would require him to step it up. He recognized that the only time the universe doesn't help you out of a problem is when it would rob you of an important chance to grow.

Conrad obviously needed this struggle to make him stronger and smarter. He would have to rise to the occasion and solve this problem on his own. You are never really alone, though; help is always there. You are often led to people who can help you, understand your challenges, and can give you some direction. Maybe that is how Conrad found me. I couldn't solve his problems for him, but I could teach him a few things that would help him find the solution.

Conrad recognized the Voice of Fear in his head and why it wanted him to feel hopeless about his situation. He started to see that he had the power to choose trust and love and escape his fear. He also realized that when he was worried about his money problems, his focus was on him, and in that state he couldn't show up for anyone else. This was probably the reason his sales weren't going too well. Even his prospects could tell he was focused on himself, not them.

This situation was Conrad's opportunity to improve his life. It was his chance to focus on others, get more organized, work harder, and become a better man. As he started to do these things, his situation quickly improved. He discovered he had a talent for serving people that he didn't know he had. As he fought his way through the challenges and practiced choosing trust and love, everything changed for the better.

The challenges you currently face serve a purpose in your life, too. If you can keep the mindset of trust as you fight your way through them, these trials will give you strength, wisdom, and empathy. They will make you stronger, kinder, and less judgmental. They will help you discover who you really are. You might not be able to see these blessings in your situation yet, but they are there and you will eventually see them.

A great procedure for finding the meaning in suffering is to get out a piece of paper and try to think of ten good things that are a result of this challenge or trial. What have you learned? Who else has this benefited? Who did this strengthen or teach to be humble? How has this created more love around you? Write down as many positives as you can.

These experiences are only locations on your journey. *They have nothing to do with your value or who you are.* They are just classes you got signed up for, and just because you are in the class, it doesn't affect your value as a person.

claritypoint: **Failures, mistakes, and difficulties are just locations on your journey through life.** They have nothing to do with who you are.

You are the one to decide how your life's challenges will affect you. You can let the challenges, trials, and mistakes drag you down into the depths of bitterness and depression if you want to. You can let them define you and serve as proof that you aren't good enough. You can use them as excuses to get you out of things you don't want to do, or cast yourself as a victim to get sympathy or love. You absolutely have that choice.

clarity**point**: **You get to decide how your challenges affect you.** You can let them depress you or you can see them accurately and use them to become a better, stronger, more loving you.

Your Voice of Fear encourages you to use trials to create drama in your life. It loves attention and self-pity, and sees being a victim as a win. Do you have a victim story? Think about the attention you get when you tell your story. Do you tell your story to make you less responsible for the choices you're making and the results you're creating? Do you use it to excuse unloving, selfish behavior? Is your story keeping you stuck and stagnant? *Is this who you want to be?*

It's time to stop making excuses and step it up. All you have to do is choose Clarity and change the way you see and experience your story. You can start by getting some paper and taking an inventory of your life experiences. Write down the difficult life experiences you have been through.

- What have you been through?
- Have you survived divorce, abuse, addiction, failure, illness, grief, or any other exciting or horrible experiences?
- Have you been a single parent or survived financial ruin?
- Have you lost a child or battled chronic illness?
- Have you experienced being lonely or feeling like you don't fit in?

Now write down some of the things you have learned or gained by surviving these experiences. You might have gained patience, trust, strength, wisdom, empathy, or compassion for other people. These experiences might have made you less judgmental and more understanding, and this knowledge is a gift.

Instead of using these experiences as excuses to wallow in self-pity, or letting them separate you from other people, you can use the knowledge you gained to bless the lives of other people. Your unique understanding about this trial can help you connect with others, *and there will be many who need your wisdom.* When you discover how to use these experiences for good, you will be empowered to make a bigger difference in the world.

Think about the bad choices or mistakes you have made. Obviously you regret these experiences, but they have taught you beautiful and important lessons. Bad choices teach some of the most powerful, life-changing lessons you will ever learn. Mistakes and bad choices teach you about forgiveness and give you compassion for others that you cannot gain any other way.

Jody's Story

Jody had made a lot of big mistakes in her life and regretted many of her choices. Because of her low self-esteem and bad choices, she and her children suffered from serious domestic abuse. Her children blamed her (and her mistakes) for most of their problems. They reminded her often of her faults, which caused her a great deal of pain. She experienced shame and guilt on a daily basis.

After learning the principles in Choosing Clarity, she gained a new understanding about who she is. She wrote a new policy that said she is a good person, a student in the classroom of life, and has absolute value in spite of her mistakes. She reviewed this policy daily and chose to believe it. I also gave her a new definition for the word *shame*. Its acronym stands for **S**hould **H**ave **A**lready **M**astered **E**verything. Jody realized it was ridiculous to think that she should have known all along what she knows now. She had done the best she could with what she knew at the time, and that was all she could do.

She also redefined the purpose of her life and realized, because of her unique and rather horrible past, that she had learned some pretty amazing lessons. She now understands people and suffering in a powerful and compassionate way.

She decided to use this gift to start a support group in her area, and she began to speak to women about domestic abuse. She forgave herself for her bad choices and realized that dwelling on them only kept her in fear.

She also realized that her children were learning important lessons about overcoming shame by watching her. If she hadn't made those mistakes, she wouldn't have had that beautiful opportunity to show her children how to rise above mistakes and forgive yourself. These are important lessons that her children needed to learn.

When Jody changed her policy about mistakes and decided to see them as learning experiences, she no longer felt guilt or angst about them. She no longer saw herself as a victim. She saw herself as a survivor who had great knowledge, love, and compassion to share. She is now proud of herself in spite of the bad choices and mistakes in her past. They were just locations on her journey, and they do not affect her value.

The world needs people who have survived mistakes, tragedies, and trials to help the rest of us through. Where would we be if Victor Frankl had never experienced what he did during the war? He wouldn't have used his experiences to benefit millions of people around the world.

The world needs you to let go of self-pity and shame regarding your life experiences, too. The world needs you to use the things you have learned for good. Stop letting your past mistakes define you and affect your value. Let go of separation and victimhood and find meaning in what you have been through.

• •

clarity**point**: **The world needs you to let go of the difficult things you have experienced and let them empower you to be more giving.**

• •

Having clearly defined policies about how you are going to see and experience your challenges and trials (before they happen) makes staying in trust and love easier. It also makes your life more peaceful and productive. Take the time to write a new official policy about how you are going to experience the rough patches in your life. Below are my personal policies to get you started.

My Personal Policies about Challenges and Trials

This is my policy about why rough, challenging, painful things happen:

I am meant to be more than I am currently being. I am here to grow and reach my potential. This process of growing and learning requires some rough experiences. I signed up for most of the difficult challenges in my life through my choices. I made these choices because there were lessons I needed to learn. But God and the universe know me too, so on occasion they sign me up for interesting challenges. But I am safely in God's hands the whole time. I am not here to lose or fail. I was born to overcome, learn, grow, and win in the end. Knowing this, I trust the process of my life even when it is difficult. I trust my way through the challenges. I know that every experience is for my good and is here to serve me.

This is my policy about failures and difficulties and how I am officially going to experience them:

All of the difficult experiences in my life — my failures, my mistakes, and my challenges — are here for a perfect reason: to teach me lessons. But they do not define me. They do not affect my value. They are just locations on my journey and interesting classes I got signed up for. They have nothing to do with who I am. My value is infinite and absolute no matter what lessons I choose or how many mistakes I make. I am still me and I am still love.

This is my official policy about how disappointments and trials affect me:

I do not let trials and disappointments break my trust in myself, God, or life. I use difficulties to become stronger, smarter, and more loving. I use everything I learn from these experiences to serve, love, and lift other people. I am a survivor and I do not give up. I do not see myself as a victim. I do not use my difficulties as excuses. I do not use them to separate me from other people. I do not need that kind of drama. I am focused on learning and loving. I trust the process of life.

Go to your notebook and create your new official policies about difficulties, failures, and disappointments.

13 - Choosing Your Thoughts

Your thoughts create and determine how you experience everything that happens in your life. We learned this from James Allen in *As a Man Thinketh*, another of my favorite books. Every feeling you have, every word you say, every choice you make, and who you eventually become are all shaped by *the way you think about yourself and the world.*

clarity**point**: **Making any change in your life starts with a change in your thinking.**

Every time a thought crosses your mind, you can ask yourself which voice it came from. Is it a trust-and-love, Clarity-based thought coming from your Voice of Truth, or a foggy, selfish, dramatic thought coming from the Voice of Fear?

The Voice of Fear is responsible for all your negative thinking. This includes anger, hate, shame, guilt, criticism, prejudice, pride, indifference, intolerance, self-pity, stress, hopelessness, lack, the need for control, rejection, jealousy, pessimism, insecurity, disappointment, suspicion, and every other negative state or emotion I might have missed.

These states are all part of the human experience, though, and you will probably get to experience all of them at some point on your journey. When this happens, allow yourself to process and feel them. Each experience is an important part of your education. Each time you experience one of these negative states, the universe is giving you the chance to understand this aspect of the human condition and decide who you want to be. You cannot avoid having these fear-based thoughts show up in your mind, but once you have experienced them and processed them for a while, you must decide to either *embrace them* or *replace them* with something better.

If you decide to embrace fear-based thinking, it will create a great deal of negative, immature, and dramatic behavior. This negativity can damage your relationships and hold you back at work. It will also bother you, depress you, and make you feel out of sync. If you consistently choose (either consciously or subconsciously) a mindset of fear, the universe might send you more things to fear. If you choose thoughts of guilt and shame, the universe might send you more situations that create guilt and shame. If you choose to dwell in fear of loss, you might create the very situation you are afraid of. If you choose to distrust people, you might subconsciously cause them to distrust you. If you choose to condemn or judge other people, you might also feel judged and condemned yourself. This is how the universe works. *You create what you think about most.*

. . . .

clarity**point**: **You create more of what you think about most.**

. . . .

If you have been a negative thinker up to this point in your life, you can begin to change that right now. You can start consciously choosing an attitude of trust and love in every moment. You can choose to think about forgiveness, gratitude, faith, compassion, understanding, optimism, and courage. You can choose to feel empowered, worthy, valued, cheerful, secure, kind, happy, loveable, calm, flexible, trusting, accepted, comfortable, confident, and peaceful. You have lots of good options to choose from.

It is not easy to choose gratitude when life is hard. It is not easy to choose to feel loved when you're alone. But you can do it. And when you consciously choose a positive mindset, the universe is bound (by universal law) to send more positive things your way. *So even when things go badly you will create solutions faster and easier if you choose trust-and-love-based, optimistic thoughts.*

I learned this lesson at a young age from my grandfather, whose motto is "Good things happen to us." I heard Grandpa Merl say this often, and he has always been one of the luckiest (most blessed) people I know. Good things happen to him all the time! Hence I decided to adopt his mindset.

Some people like to believe that choosing your attitude isn't possible in some situations, and that you can't help feeling the way you feel. But this is a cop-out. They are just looking for an excuse so they don't have to be responsible for choosing their attitude and the outcomes in their life. But it is not truth. You have the power to choose your attitude in any situation. If Viktor Frankl could do it, we can too. It is the one choice, the one power that no one can take away from you, *but you can give this power away.* You can decide to let other people and situations make you feel a certain way if you want to. The universe will not force a positive mindset on you. You have to choose it.

I have worked with many people over the years who struggled with basically hopeless problems – *negative situations that for the most part could not be fixed or changed.* In these situations there was always one very powerful thing they could change – their perspective. They could make a fundamental change in how they saw themselves and their lives, and this always made the situation more bearable. They made this fundamental change stick by changing their official policies about it.

clarity**point**: **Just changing the way you think can change the most important thing in your life – the way you feel about yourself.**

Barbara's Story

Barbara was one of the most amazing people I've ever worked with. When she came to me for coaching, she was in bad shape. She had some serious health problems that had caused her to gain a great deal of weight, and this had made it difficult for her to clean her house. Her house was now a disaster area. (I think she would agree with that description.) Barbara was so embarrassed by her situation that she had cut herself off from the people in her life. She wouldn't let family or friends visit her and she had stopped visiting them. She felt safer staying home alone.

The first thing we did in coaching was talk about who Barbara really was and why she was here on this journey. Barbara wrote some new policies about God, the purpose of life, and what it takes to have value as a human being. She really grasped the idea that her value came from her love.

We also talked about her inner truth and the many talents and gifts she had. Barbara was truly an amazing soul, but her Voice of Fear had worked really hard to convince her that she wasn't. Barbara was one of the most loving souls I have ever met, but she had a really mean Voice of Fear. It had done a good job of making her feel ashamed of herself. It had convinced her she had no value at all.

Through coaching, Barbara started to recognize her fear-based thoughts for what they were — lies, fog, and illusions. When she understood their agenda — to rob the world of her love — it made her angry. She was not going to let fear stop her from reaching out to others anymore.

There were many things in her life (like her house and her weight) that she could not easily change, but there was one important thing that she could change – how she felt about herself. Barbara could also look at her house and her weight from a new trust-and-love perspective and refuse to let them affect her self-esteem. She could choose to see her situation as a class she got signed up for instead of letting it determine her value. She could change how she interacted with other people, too. She could choose to base her self-esteem on her love and see herself as an irreplaceable, divine, and amazing soul instead of basing her value on extrinsic stuff like her weight that didn't mean anything anyway.

As Barbara chose better thoughts based in trust and love, she felt more motivated than she had in a long time. She also realized she had been suffering from a fear of success. Fear of success is fear of the responsibilities and commitments that come with raising the bar and shooting higher. She thought that if she started cleaning her house, everyone would expect her to do it perfectly forever, so she was safer not doing it at all. The Clarity Formula helped her see that her value wasn't on the line either way. Once failure was off the table, most of her fear went away. She didn't have to be perfect to be good enough. Her value was infinite and absolute whether she cleaned the house or not. Now she could start working on it and feel safe in the process. So she turned on some music and did as much cleaning as she could each day. She also started singing again, something else she had given up.

The best part of her story is that Barbara started reaching out to family, friends, and neighbors again. She invited them over and went to see them, and their lives were blessed by her company. She was really good at edifying people and making them feel valued. She also had the gift of wisdom, and soon became everyone's source for good advice.

Barbara couldn't change much about her situation, but she could change what was happening inside her head. She changed the way she valued herself. She trusted God about her value and her life, and chose to lift and love the people around her. Doing these things made the last years of her life rich. Changing how you see your life and how you think about yourself is the critical first step to changing everything else.

The following are important principles of truth that will help you create some policies about healthy thinking:

claritypoint: **Your happiness does not depend on your situation or your results; it depends on how you choose to think about yourself, your situation, and your results.**

claritypoint: **Your success is not measured by what you do, earn, or create here on earth; it is measured by who you become on the inside, what you learn, and how you love.**

You have the power to change your thinking and your life. When fear-based thoughts enter your mind, you can replace them as fast as you can with gratitude, trust, or love. You can use the Clarity Formula to help do this. Below are my personal policies about healthy thinking. You can use them to get you started writing your own.

My Personal Policies about Choosing My Thoughts

This is my official policy about my power to choose my thoughts:

I understand the power of my thoughts. They are the roots of everything I create in my life. I understand that I have the power to choose my attitude and mindset in every situation. I can't control the situations that show up in my life, but I always get to decide how I experience each situation. No one can make me feel any certain way. If I get angry, it is because I am choosing to get angry. I am the one in control, and I consciously recognize and claim that power. My happiness does not depend on my situation. It depends on how I choose to feel about myself in every situation.

This is my policy about experiencing fear-based emotions:

I am here to experience every human emotion possible because each is teaching me something. When bad things happen I allow myself to feel and process what I am feeling, but I do not embrace negative thoughts about my situation. I can feel the Voice of Fear encouraging me to dwell there, though. It also encourages all kinds of bad behavior. It makes me want to react and get angry or create unnecessary drama. After a while I have to decide what I want in my life and who I want to be. In each situation I step back and run through the Clarity Formula. This helps me clearly see what is best for me and the people I love.

I am responsible for my thinking, my attitude, and my mindset. I choose to be optimistic and hopeful in every situation. This isn't always easy to do, but the only other option makes things worse. I choose trust, optimism, and love.

Write some policies about positive thinking. Officially decide how you will handle the negative thoughts that show up in your head. Then read all your policies daily until they are internalized.

14 – Communicating with Love

In this chapter you will learn how to apply the principles you've learned so far to improve the way you communicate with other people. Success in your career and the quality of your relationships at home are completely dependent on your ability to communicate well, because communication is the foundation of good relationships.

I will teach you a simple formula you can use in *every conversation you have with anyone.* It is completely universal and will never let you down. This formula creates mutually validating conversations that make everyone involved feel valued, honored, and respected. If you know how to have mutually validating conversations, there is almost no problem or situation you can't resolve.

The first step to having mutually validating conversations is to choose to see the other people or person involved as the same as you. Make sure you are not seeing them as better than you or worse than you. *(This is also one of the Clarity Formula steps we discussed earlier.)*

· ·

clarity**point**:   **Many of your conversations have a fear-based dynamic to them.** You often cast yourself as the good guy (strong and powerful) or the bad guy (weak and scared). You either allow people to talk down to you or you talk down to them. These dynamics do not create good conversations.

· ·

If you have cast the other person as the bad guy (seeing them as worse than you), they will subconsciously feel this before you even say a word, and they will get defensive before the conversation even begins. Their subconscious can feel your fear-based attitude towards them. If you see them as better than you, they will feel this, too. They will feel your lack of confidence in yourself and they will subconsciously lose respect for you before the conversation even starts. If this happens they might talk down to you, walk on you, or take advantage of you.

Seeing other people as the same as you lays the foundation for a conversation that respects and honors both people as equals. An amazing thing happens when you treat people as equals – even your employees or children; *they begin to feel respected and safe with you, which makes them more cooperative, open, and easy to work with.*

. . . .

clarity**point**: **When you show another person that you honor and respect them and see them as the same as you, you can have productive, open, and cooperative conversations.**

. . . .

Making the other person feel valued, honored, and respected should be your number one goal in every conversation. After you have made the person feel valued and cared about, you can address your agenda or purpose for the conversation. The Communication Formula I am about to teach you shows exactly how to do this.

. . . .

clarity**point**: **When a person feels appreciated for their infinite and absolute value, you can then communicate about any issue and you will have their cooperation and respect.**

. . . .

Before I teach you the Communication Formula, I need to define the word *stuff* in the formula. I call everything inside your head (your thoughts, feelings, beliefs, ideas, opinions, values, fears, and concerns) "*your stuff.*" I refer to everything in the other person's head (their thoughts, feelings, beliefs, ideas, opinions, values, fears, and concerns) as "*their stuff.*"

The formula produces amazing conversations because when you value another person's stuff first, they are much more open to hearing about and honoring your stuff.

clarity**point**: **Honoring and respecting someone's stuff (their thoughts and feelings) shows you value them.**

Remember the old saying *"They don't care what you know, until they know that you care"?* This principle is the basis for the Communication Formula. If you show the other person you value them first, by respecting and honoring their thoughts and feelings and their right to have them, you create a conversation in which you can respectfully share your thoughts and feelings and they will be open to hearing you.

This amazing formula works in every conversation you will ever have. It is universally applicable even though you might not use all of the steps in every conversation. It might take some practice to get used to communicating this way, though. You might want to write the formula on a card and carry it with you everywhere you go or take a picture of it and use it as the wallpaper on your phone.

If you have a difficult conversation in which you forget to use the formula, take some time to replay the conversation in your mind and imagine how you could have used the formula and handled things differently. Visualization is a powerful way to practice and it helps you internalize the steps even more.

I recommend that you think of someone you need to have a conversation with and imagine how you might handle that specific situation as you read through the steps.

The Communication Formula

Goal: To edify each person I talk to and make them feel valued, which builds a relationship of trust in which respectful communication can happen.

1. I choose to see this person as the same as me.

2. **I set my stuff aside up front.** I set my thoughts, feelings, ideas, opinions, beliefs, values, fears, and concerns aside so I can focus on validating the other person first.

3. **I ask questions about their stuff. I listen and validate them.** I ask questions about their thoughts, feelings, opinions, ideas, fears, and concerns. I listen attentively to whatever they say. I do not agree or disagree at this point. I honor and respect their right to think and feel the way they do.

    Validating means honoring their right to see the world the way they see it and have their unique viewpoint. When I validate them it shows I value who they are.

4. **I ask permission to share my stuff.** I never give advice, share my opinion, or tell my stories without asking for permission first. I respect other people enough to ask if they would be open or willing to hear what I have to say. I wait for their permission before I say a word about my own stuff.

    Here are some examples of permission questions:

    - "Would you be open to some advice on that?"

- "Would you be willing to let me share my perspective, even if it's a little different from yours?"
- "Would you be open to hearing about something that happened to me?"
- Would you be willing to stay quiet and not respond until I have finished?" (Sometimes you must get specific about what you are asking for.)

5. **If I have permission to share, I speak for myself using "I" statements, not "you" statements. I focus on their future behavior more than their past behavior.** I use "I" statements because I can only speak for my own feelings and experiences. When I use "you" statements it triggers defensiveness. Instead of talking about past behavior (which this person cannot change), I focus on the future behavior I'd like to see. When I do this the other person responds more positively.

Following these five simple steps can change the way you communicate forever. You also create more win/win solutions to problems because you come from love, not fear, ego, or the need to be right. If you use the formula consistently, all your conversations will be more productive.

Sara's Story

Sara received a call from the high school informing her that her son had skipped a class. She was furious and scared. This situation triggered her fear of loss and her fear of failure as a mother. She had some strong feelings about ditching school, and her gut reaction was to yell at her son, but because she had recently learned the Communication Formula, she reigned in her fear and chose to try it.

The first step was making sure she saw her son as the same as her. This meant she couldn't talk down to him. She had to see him as an adult and talk to him as an equal. Next Sara set her stuff (her thoughts and feelings) about his ditching school aside. She decided to listen to her son's side of the story before she said a word. (Thinking, asking questions, and listening before you speak is always a good idea.) She wanted to edify him and show him he was loved even if he was in trouble. She made a commitment to show him he was valued, honored, and respected before she said anything.

When her son came home, she asked him if they could chat for a minute. She explained about the call from the school and asked if he would be willing to tell her what happened. (He was amazed she wasn't yelling.) He explained that his friend had gotten sick after lunch and didn't have a way to get home. Sara's son had offered to skip class and drive him home. He knew it was wrong, but he felt that showing up for his friend was more important.

Sara could tell her son was sincere. He had always been a soft-hearted person who really cared about other people. She listened and told him she understood why he made the decision he made. (She validated him.) She also asked questions about how he felt about his grades, what he thought about missing school, and when he thought missing school was appropriate. The more time she spent on Step 3, the more she learned about her son, and the more valued her son felt. She kept him talking for quite a while.

Then she asked him a permission question. "Would you be open to letting me share some of my thoughts about this situation?" He was a little nervous about this, but he said, "Sure."

She said, "I love you, Son, and I really want you to be successful in school and life. I get scared when I hear about your skipping school because I am afraid you won't have the bright future I want for you. The next time something like this happens, would you be open to calling me and explaining the situation up front so I won't feel like you're sneaking around and get scared? Would you be open to that moving forward?"

He said, "Sure, Mom. That would feel better to me, too."

Did you notice she used "I" statements and focused on future behavior, not past behavior? That was the right way to share her stuff.

When Sara shared this experience with me I was a little suspicious about the boy's story. But even if her son was lying about why he skipped school, she still handled it the right way. It is usually better to trust people and be wrong than not to trust them and be wrong (though you should listen to your gut in each situation).

I also think treating people as better than they actually are can inspire them to want to be better, while treating them with distrust or as a bad person can actually encourage more bad behavior. When you see the best in someone, you often push them in that direction. *They want to live up to your highest opinion of them.*

claritypoint: **Encouragement is the most effective way to change someone's behavior.** When you see the best in them you encourage them to become that and they will want to live up to your high opinion of them.

Building a relationship of trust is also very important. By asking her son questions and validating his right to think and feel the way he did, Sara showed her son that she valued him more than she cared about his behavior. When you show someone they are valued first, they handle it better when you disagree with their ideas.

Sara was able to escape her fears about losing her son and feeling like a failure and instead focus on love for her son. Following the Communication Formula made this happen. It also made her feel wise, capable, loving, and in control.

Now it's your turn. Practice the Communication Formula in every conversation you have this week. Write it down as an official procedure for handling most of the conversations you have, especially the difficult ones. Make communicating this way and validating other people your official policy. Review the formula often to keep it fresh in your mind.

My Personal Policy and Procedure about Communication

This is my policy about my communication:

Every conversation I have is a chance to show another human being that they are valued. I take every opportunity I can to validate, listen to, respect, and honor other people. I ask lots of questions and show people I am interested in them. This shows them they are valued and even lets them feel God's love for them through me.

This is my procedure for handling difficult conversations:

Some conversations make me nervous and trigger my fear of not being good enough or my fear of loss. When this happens I run through the Clarity Formula to escape my fear and take my value out of the equation. Next I make sure I am seeing the other person as the same as me and trust that this experience is in my life for a reason to teach me something.

Once I am in Clarity, I am ready to have the conversation using the Communication Formula.

I set my stuff aside up front. In every conversation I show people I value them by asking questions about their stuff and listen to them. Even if I don't agree with them, I validate their right to see the world the way they see it.

I respectfully ask permission before I say anything. It is my official policy to never give advice or share my story or my ideas without asking permission to do so first. This creates relationships of trust in which good communication can happen.

I use "I" statements, not "you" statements, so people don't get defensive. And I focus on future behavior, not past behavior, because they can only change the future. This also makes people feel respected and valued. Sometimes the other person realizes they have more to say at this point, and I start the formula over again. If I stick to the steps of the formula, I can handle any conversation and create a solution to any problem.

I always look for win/win compromises and find solutions that honor the needs of both parties. Sometimes this isn't possible, though. In those situations I make sure the other person feels valued even though I disagree with them. This is not about winning; my ego doesn't need to win. It is about standing up for what I believe while honoring other people and what they believe, too.

Record your new policies and procedures about communication about communication in your notebook.

15 – Edifying Other People

Every day the universe gives you opportunities to set aside your fears, choose trust and love, and be a giver. The most powerful way to be a giver is to edify other people. I use the word *edify* often, by which I mean to validate another person's worth by honoring them, respecting who they are now, and encouraging them to be their highest, best self.

The most significant way you can edify another person is to see them accurately as the same as you, listen to them, and honor their right to their own thoughts and feelings. You must also give them permission to be a work in progress or a student in the classroom of life, just like you. Seeing other people accurately doesn't happen by accident, though; you must choose it. If you don't consciously choose to see others as the same as you, your subconscious mind will automatically see them with fear – as better than or worse than you.

Consciously choosing to see people accurately is one of the most important and fundamental changes you can make to change your life and relationships forever.

Margo's Story

Margo and Ben were not happy. Ben was working long hours and travelling quite a bit for his job. Margo worked part time and had a full time job at home with the children. They were both tired and they both felt unloved and unappreciated.

When Ben was home he wanted to rest. Margo thought that when Ben was home he should be ready to help out with the kids and give her a break. She was tired of doing everything alone. She had tried to explain what she was feeling and what she needed from him, but he didn't seem to care, and nothing ever changed.

When Margo came to me for coaching, she was thinking about leaving Ben. She was the only one interested in getting help and she honestly believed Ben was the problem in their marriage. I recommended we try changing her behavior first to see if that would change things. *(If you want to change anything in your life, you have to change YOU first.)*

I asked her to assess whether she was showing up with fear or love in the relationship. Was she focused more on getting what she needed or giving love and validation to Ben?

She could see that she wasn't focused on giving love and validation at all. Love was not happening in their relationship because neither of them was giving any. They were both in fear and focused on getting. *This is what fear does.* If you are afraid that your spouse doesn't love you, it prevents you from being loving towards your spouse. Remember that you can't do fear and love at the same time.

Margo recognized immediately that her thoughts were mostly fear-based and focused on her. She also recognized that she could not blame that on Ben; that she was the one in control of her fear and how it affected her behavior. Margo also admitted that her Voice of Fear was a drama queen. It told her that everything Ben said or did meant he didn't love her. *The Voice of Fear inaccurately applies your core fear to everything that happens. You have to watch for that.*

clarity**point**:   **Your Voice of Fear applies your core fear to every situation.** It tells you that you aren't good enough or loved in every situation. This feels accurate, but it isn't.

Margo realized that she was applying her core fear all over the place and that this was not mature behavior. Every time Ben was grouchy, she thought that meant he didn't love her because she wasn't good enough. Through coaching she came to see that his grouchy behavior was about *his fears about himself*, not about her **at all**. It was time to grow up.

She worked hard to get control of her thoughts. She learned that she could choose to see each situation accurately if she worked at it. Next she worked on forgiving Ben and herself for their past bad behavior. They had both behaved badly and they both deserved forgiveness. She also realized that if she continued to attack Ben for his faults, she would never feel good about herself either. When you condemn others you subconsciously don't like yourself and tend toward low self-esteem. Choosing forgiveness helped get her heart in the right place and she wiped the slate clean for both of them.

The problem was that Ben still wasn't doing the things she wanted him to do, and they still weren't communicating well. It was time to use the Communication Formula. I explained to Margo that if she asked questions and listened to Ben's feelings first, she would make him feel validated and valued, and he would be in a better place to hear her feelings. If they followed the formula, they could start building each other up in their conversations instead of tearing each other down every time they talked.

The next day she asked Ben if they could set aside some time to talk when they would not be interrupted by the kids. He nervously agreed, but was obviously concerned that the conversation would turn into a fight. At the appointed time she made sure she was seeing Ben as the same as her; that she was not casting him as the bad guy and herself as the good guy in their relationship; they were both the same. This was hard to do because her Voice of Fear still wanted to see Ben as the problem, but she refused to let it. She gave Ben (and herself) permission to be a scared, struggling, divine, amazing student in the classroom of life.

Then she set her feelings about the relationship aside. She committed to focusing on edifying Ben first. She asked Ben how he was feeling about their marriage. He was not sure if he could really speak his truth at first. *In the past it would have elicited a lot of drama and was never worth it.* She had to assure him that she was in a good, calm place and really wanted to understand how he felt. Then he opened up. He told her that he felt unappreciated and unloved. He felt she was hard to please and he could never do anything right. He thought at times that she was selfish and only wanted him around for his paycheck and as a weekend babysitter.

This was difficult for her to hear. At times she really wanted to interrupt him and defend herself. But she didn't do it. She was determined to validate him and not make the conversation about her. *(This is not easy, but it can be done.)*

He was shocked. He was not used to loving and mature behavior from his wife. It meant the world to him that she really cared how he felt. She listened for quite a while and only spoke to ask more questions. The longer she listened and let him talk, the more valued he felt.

Then an amazing thing happened. Ben's coldness started to melt away because Margo cared enough to listen and understand him. Ben realized on his own that he had not been very helpful or kind to Margo recently. Without her saying a word he recognized that she was carrying a lot on her shoulders, and that he could do more to help. He apologized for not being a better husband. She apologized for not being a better wife. All of a sudden each of them had a soft heart. They listened and talked for the first time in years.

At one point Margo asked Ben (in a permission question) if he would be willing to hear some of her feelings, and he was. She had earned it by validating him first. She was careful to use "I" statements instead of attacks, and her feelings didn't offend him. They both made a commitment to be less scared about not being loved, and to be more loving. All their problems weren't solved in one conversation, but they knew how to have validating conversations and began to work it all out. I am happy to report that they are still together.

Here are a few other tips that can help you have effective, edifying conversations. You might want to make some of these into policies.

Tips for Edifying Other People

- Do not have a conversation if you or the other person is tired, hungry, sick, or grouchy. Sometimes you need to get a good night's sleep before effective communication can occur.
- Ask the person if they would be open to talking with you. This respectful permission question is the best way to start.
- If necessary, set aside a time and place to have this conversation, in private, and when you will not be interrupted.
- Have compassion and put yourself in the other person's shoes. Imagine how they feel and what is going on in their life. What are they afraid of? What do they need? This will help you see them and the situation accurately.

- Tell them you will not interrupt them when they answer your questions. This is especially important if you have not been a good listener in the past. *It can take a while to earn their trust back.* Promise them you will keep your mouth shut and then do it.
- While on Step 3 of the Communication Formula (asking questions and listening), do not agree or disagree with what they say. Just validate and honor their right to have their thoughts and feelings.
- Do not go to Step 4 unless absolutely necessary. It is ideal if you can just ask questions and listen. You might be able to guide them to discover what you were going to tell them without your ever saying a thing.

Edifying other people requires keeping your mouth shut most of the time. For some of you this will be easy; for others it will be like holding back the tide. *Some of us have a tendency to talk too much.* You might do this because you need the validation you get when you talk and other people listen to you. Does this sound familiar?

Ask yourself how often you feel the need to talk and share your thoughts or opinions. Do you ever dominate a conversation or meeting? Do you tell too many of your own stories? Is there any chance you are subconsciously trying to get validation? Do you feel important and valued when you talk?

The problem with this behavior is that it dishonors other people. It is not consistent or worthy of the amazing person you really are.

clarity**point**: **You feel better about yourself when you listen more than you talk.** When you listen to others you create self-esteem because you are being the best you.

If you want to change your life or career fast, stop talking and start listening to and edifying people everywhere you go. Be the love in your home. Be the love at your office. Be the love in your community. And do this by asking more questions and doing more listening. When you do this and focus on lifting other people in every situation, even more of your fear disappears. Below is my personal policy on edifying others. It might help you write your own.

My Personal Policy about Edifying Other People

I am here to learn and love. The best way I can show people that I love and value them is by listening to their thoughts and feelings. It is my official policy to listen more than I talk. I choose to be a master question-asker and give positive attention and validation to people everywhere I go. I always ask questions and listen to the other person before I say anything. I do this because it is very important to me that I edify my fellow human beings as much as possible. They deserve to be treated this way. I want them to feel God's love for them through me.

Being this kind of person also helps my self-esteem. I like who I am when I am being a force for love in this world.

Create an official policy about edifying other people and remember, to read through all your policies every day. Make edifying other people your official policy and you will be amazed by how your life and your relationships improve.

16 – Handling Mistreatment

Almost every day someone will offend you, hurt you, criticize you, or tick you off in some way. How you handle these situations greatly affects how you feel about yourself. If you struggle to forgive other people or are easily offended, you will live in fear, have low self-esteem, and fear judgment from other people.

Embracing anger, hurt, or even dislike toward people who mistreat you *increases the amount of subconscious fear you have about not being good enough.* Please read that again; it is an important universal truth.

• •

clarity**point**: **If you spend your energy condemning and judging the people who mistreat you, it puts you in a condemning and judging mindset that subconsciously makes you feel condemned and judged, too.**

• •

Think about this for a minute. You have probably not related being mad at other people with low self-esteem, but the two are inseparably connected. Hate and judgment are tied to the belief that other people can be "not good enough," and if *they* can be not good enough (if that is possible), then *you* can, too. If you can't see their infinite value, you won't be able to see your own either.

Earlier we established that you are here primarily to learn to love. *That means your number one task here is to forgive yourself and the people who mistreat you.* You must learn to do this if you want to experience real happiness and peace in this life. You must do this if you want to feel accepted, valued, and safe. The only way to feel innocent and worthy *is to give innocence and worthiness to other people*. If you choose to hold on to hate, judgment, and resentment towards other people, you are also choosing to feel unsafe, unvalued, and judged yourself, because *you get what you give.*

I know that forgiveness is tough, so I will teach you a different way to experience mistreatment. When you see it from a more accurate perspective, it won't seem so hard.

. . . .

clarity**point**: **Your ability to forgive others determines how much happiness you create in your life.**

. . . .

You must first understand that the Voice of Fear in your head loves the drama that is created when you choose to be angry, hurt, or sad. The Voice of Fear feels important and even significant when there is drama and mistreatment going on in your life. It likes the attention and sympathy mistreatment brings. It also thinks you have to stay angry with those who mistreat you to protect yourself from them, but that isn't true. You don't need to stay angry to be safe. You need to be in Clarity about your value and your life so you can see yourself and the situation accurately. That is what makes you feel safe.

When others mistreat you, use the Clarity Formula to be sure you are seeing the situation, yourself, and the other person accurately. Remember that your value isn't on the line and your life is the perfect classroom journey for you. Then choose to see the other person involved as the same as you, and choose an edifying and loving mindset towards yourself and them. This doesn't mean you will trust them or allow them to further mistreat you. And it might even mean loving yourself enough to leave the situation. But running through the Clarity Formula will help you remember that every experience of being mistreated is a lesson that is in your life to teach you something. *Most of the time it is there to teach you love at a deeper level.*

The Clarity Formula also reminds you that no one can really diminish you. They might hurt you financially or take things from you, but they can't make you less than who you are. *Your value is unchangeable no matter what they do or say.* Their value is also unchangeable no matter what they do and say because you are the same and have the same infinite value.

Forgiving mistreatment and responding with love becomes easier when you remember these truths. But I am not talking about forgiving people in the traditional sense; I am talking about seeing the person and their value accurately and seeing yourself and your value accurately so that there is really nothing to forgive – the whole situation is just a lesson.

Harold Kushner, a Jewish rabbi and the author of the amazing book *How Good Do We Have to Be?* said, "Forgiveness is correcting the misconception that anyone can harm us." Think about what that means. If you are in trust about your value, then nothing anyone thinks, does, or says about you can take away from who you are. And if they can't harm you or diminish you, is there really anything to forgive?

Think back on some of the mistreatment situations you have experienced in your life. What have these experiences shown you about yourself? What have they taught you? How have they made you a better person? What good have they created in the world? Can you trust the process of life, embrace these experiences as perfect lessons, and let go of your fear, hurt, and pain around them? Can you choose to forgive and let go of the need to condemn so you won't experience fear about your own value? *(You might want to take a minute to answer those questions on paper.)*

Work on seeing the people who have mistreated you as the same as you. This does not mean dismissing their bad behavior or letting them continue to abuse you. It just means owning the truth that you both have the same infinite value. They are not perfect and neither are you. You might not have done what they did, but you have done other bad things over the course of your life in your process of learning. You have been selfish at times and you have said unkind things. Owning this brings compassion and Clarity to the situation. The other person is not the bad guy and you are not the good guy. In reality you are both struggling, scared, divine, amazing students in the classroom of life. You are both good and bad at times, and neither can cast the first stone. (I realize they could be more bad than you, but the point is *we are all imperfect.*)

Owning your mistakes makes it easier to give other people permission to be flawed, struggling students in the classroom of life and let go of your anger towards them. *You cannot expect perfection in other people while at the same time allowing imperfections in yourself.* It's a two-way street. Either we are all infinite and absolute or none of us are. Either we are all forgiven or none of us are. How do you want to live?

Everyone is here in the classroom of life to learn and grow, and we are all "right on track" in our personal process of becoming. So you must let others be good enough when they are. You must give them permission to be works in progress with much to learn. Most of their mistakes *and yours* were born of fear and misconception. Most of us are not "being evil" when we mistreat others or make mistakes. We are being scared, misinformed, ill-educated, confused, lost, and sometimes stupid, but we are not intending evil. We are just scared and blind.

What we deserve for these mistakes is truth, education, correction, Clarity, and learning. We really need to gain knowledge, correct our misconceptions, and start seeing things more accurately. We need the classroom of life to learn from our bad choices and past mistakes. A learning process would fix this, change us, and resolve these situations better than being judged, condemned, or punished would. I believe God and the universe are more interested in learning than in punishment. What do you think?

I believe we will all get the correction, learning, and Clarity we need at some point in our journey *because education is what we are here for.* You can rest assured that those who mistreat you will eventually learn lessons from their choices. But you and the other person are both safe, whole, and forgiven the entire time because life is a classroom, not a test.

clarity**point**: **Seeing others as works in progress, and life as a classroom, makes forgiveness easier.** If you want to create more happiness and peace in your life, see others accurately and become a good forgiver.

Helen's Story

Helen was very frustrated and disappointed with her husband. He was constantly doing selfish things that made her angry, and he was really quite mean to her. Helen had put up with this behavior for thirty-five years, and she had reached her breaking point. Each week in coaching she rehearsed a long list of her husband's mistakes. *(He was apparently impossible to live with and couldn't do anything right.)* But I could also see that Helen's behavior was a large part of the problem, too. She was extremely critical of him and said unkind things to him. I could also see that Helen had low self-esteem and a lot of fear about not being good enough.

Helen needed to take a good hard look at herself, her subconscious policies, and her behavior towards her husband. In coaching she realized that her thoughts about him and herself were mostly fear-based and negative, and that these thoughts were making the problems worse. She also recognized that she liked to be critical of her husband and was definitely casting him as the bad guy so she could feel like the good guy.

It took some convincing for her to see that her critical thoughts were the problem in the marriage and that her negative thoughts were not her husband's fault. He couldn't make her be angry; she chose to be angry, and she chose to be angry over a lot of really small things. Helen did this because she was scared. The Voice of Fear in her head said that making her husband the bad guy would make her feel better; but it didn't.

Over time Helen started to see that her husband wasn't as horribly bad as her Voice of Fear told her he was. It conveniently overlooked his good behavior and focused only on the bad, which allowed her to cast him as the bad guy and feel right about it. After a bit of coaching, Helen finally accepted that she was in control of her thinking, feeling, and behavior; that she could choose to be a loving person no matter how her husband behaved. She could see that this would take a lot of maturity and wisdom, but was more consistent with the person she wanted to be. We also worked on her self-esteem and she became able to trust that she had absolute value.

Helen could also see that when her husband was mean it was usually because she had said something critical to him first. This was difficult for her to accept because the Voice of Fear did not want to see her bad behavior; it only wanted to focus on his. She liked the story that cast him as the bad guy so much she didn't want to see the truth.

After a few weeks of coaching Helen realized that being mean back is never justified. It always makes you as bad as (and the same as) the other person. It doesn't matter who was bad first. If we get even more accurate, no one is bad at all. We are all just scared, and our fear creates bad behavior that is way beneath who we really are. We need to get out of fear and into trust so we can start being our real selves – love.

clarity**point**: **There are no good guys and no bad guys. We are all struggling, scared, divine, amazing human beings in process.** If you focus on another person's bad behavior, you will miss the lesson. The situation is here to help you become more loving.

Helen realized she was going to have to change her thinking and her behavior if she wanted to have a good relationship with her husband. She was going to have to be more loving if she wanted more love back. She had to let go of her Voice of Fear's need to be right, and choose love instead.

As she learned to communicate using the Communication Formula, her husband's behavior also started to change. When he felt respected and valued, he respected and valued her back.

The most difficult part of this process for Helen was forgiving her husband for past wrongs and letting him be a work in progress. He was clearly in a different place in his process of learning than she was, but he had the right to be where he was. He deserved the chance to learn at his own pace. He also deserved to be treated with love and respect now, even though he had a lot to learn (the same thing she wanted).

It was not easy for Helen to let go of her anger and resentment against her husband. The Voice of Fear really wanted to hold on to it. She could feel her ego side encouraging angry thoughts about him all the time. Seeing him as the bad guy was a hard habit to break. She had to pay careful attention to her thinking to catch her fear-based thoughts and replace them with Clarity, but slowly Helen began to change her mind and her heart.

She more often chose love, accuracy, and forgiveness instead of criticism and blame. This made her feel better about her husband and herself. When you choose trust and love over fear, your self-esteem always improves. Every day Helen chose to edify her husband, see the good in him, and encourage him instead of tearing him down for every mistake. She is not perfect at it, but she is fighting the battle to choose trust and love.

Real forgiveness is about fundamentally changing the way you see a situation. It is about clearing away the fog of fear and seeing the situation and the people involved accurately. It means acknowledging that there is really nothing to forgive because you are bulletproof and can't be diminished anyway. It means seeing the experience as a lesson, embracing what it is here to teach you, and choosing to be more loving toward yourself and others.

clarity**point**: **Forgiveness is the process of changing your mind about a situation and seeing the people involved accurately.**

You can decide now – ahead of time – how you are going to process the next mistreatment situation that shows up in your life. Below is a procedure that can help you see situations of mistreatment accurately. Go through the questions whenever you are offended and see if they change how you feel.

The Forgiveness Formula

Get out a piece of paper and answer the following in detail:

1. What is the mistreatment you are currently angry or hurt about?

2. Why do you feel your anger or hurt is justified?

3. How is your anger or hurt affecting you and the other person?

4. Do you understand that holding on to this is self-inflicted suffering affects the way you feel about yourself?

5. Does it hurt the other person if you stay angry, hurt, or miserable? Does it affect you?

6. Put yourself in the other person's shoes. What was going on in their world at the time of the offense? What were they afraid of? What did they need?

7. How can you see them as the same as you? Do you remember that they have the same value you have no matter what they do?

8. How did you contribute or respond to this situation? Were you loving and kind? How did your behavior contribute to the problem?

9. What does this experience show you about yourself? What might it be here to teach you? How has it created some good in your life?

10. How can you step it up and be a better person? How can you choose love and forgiveness for yourself and the other person?

You can download a worksheet with the Forgiveness Formula from my website, www.claritypointcoaching.com. There is also a High Level Forgiveness Formula on the website if you are ready to go there.

Every mistreatment experience shows up to give you the opportunity to learn love at a deeper level. So if your happiness is being destroyed by anger, hurt, or the need to cast another person as the bad guy, use the Clarity Formula and let it go. Even if you feel justified in casting them as the bad guy, let it go. I know it won't be easy because the Voice of Fear strongly encourages you to hold on to anger to defend and protect yourself; let it go anyway.

You don't need to defend yourself because you cannot be diminished. *Defensiveness doesn't protect you; it actually makes you feel more vulnerable and unsafe.* In protecting yourself you embrace the idea that you can be hurt, and this only creates more fear in your life. If you embrace fear and judgment you are choosing to live in fear and judgment.

If you choose to let go of the need to protect and defend yourself and put down your defenses because you understand you cannot be hurt, you will actually feel safer. *Security comes from trust in your value.* When you choose to feel bulletproof, infinite, and absolute all the time, no defense is ever necessary.

Choose forgiveness because it is the kind of person you want to be and because you want to feel safe and loved. You will find that living this way – seeing all people as infinite and absolute – feels amazing. You can choose to feel bulletproof and safe all the time and let all judgment and resentment go.

But if someone is verbally, emotionally, or physically abusing you in any way, or if they are toxic because their own fears are poisoning them, love yourself enough to get out of the relationship or the situation posthaste. *There are some people it is better to love and forgive from afar.* There are times when getting out of a bad relationship and holding the other person accountable for their bad behavior is the *loving* thing to do. You are actually *not* doing them a favor by allowing them to treat you badly. They need to learn that their bad behavior is not acceptable, and sometimes the universe chooses you to teach this.

You should never accept or allow abusive mistreatment. You should love yourself in the same way that you love and value other people. This means that you will always take care of yourself. You will forgive small mistreatments and let them go because they don't really matter, and you will stand up for yourself against big mistreatments and never get walked on. You won't get offended by every little thing, but you also won't be a doormat.

The good news is that your Voice of Truth (your spirit side) knows which is appropriate in each situation. Sometimes your perfect lesson is to forgive the offense, and sometimes the lesson is about having the strength to stand up for yourself, speak up, or get out of the relationship. Only you will know what is right for you in each moment.

Having said that, even if you leave an abusive situation you will still need to forgive so you can stop suffering and live in peace. You must acknowledge that the other person's value is infinite and absolute just like yours. You must give them permission to be a work in progress and not take anything they did personally. You must remember that their mistreatment was more about their own self-hate than it was about you.

. . . .

clarity**point**: **Forgiving those who have mistreated you is one of the most important lessons you are here to learn.** You can use the Clarity Formula to see people and situations accurately and trust the journey, which will make forgiveness much easier.

. . . .

It will also help you to remember these points from earlier in the book:

. . . .

clarity**point**: **Fear is the root cause of most bad behavior.** When others behave badly, it is not about you; it is about their fear of not being good enough or their fear of loss.

. . . .

. . . .

clarity**point**: **All bad behavior is really a request for love, attention, or validation.**

. . . .

Forgiveness does not mean eschewing justice, though, and it does not mean you will trust the other person again. You should not allow this person to walk on you or take advantage of you. You should create and enforce boundaries, but you should do it all from trust and love, knowing that you can't really be hurt.

It will take some work to fully understand what this new mindset about mistreatment looks like. But it will get easier as you practice the formulas in *Choosing Clarity*. When you really internalize these principles, you will find it gets easier to let go of anger, judgment, and defensiveness, and choose love.

Below is my personal policy when mistreated. I hope it will give you some ideas for writing your own.

My Personal Policies and Procedure about Handling Mistreatment

This is my policy about seeing other people and their bad behavior accurately:

> It is my official policy to see other people as the same as me. They are scared, struggling, amazing, divine students in the classroom of life, just like me. I remember that their bad behavior is usually about their own fears; it is not usually about me. Even when they attack me, it is usually about their fear.

I give them permission to be works in progress. I understand that most of the time "they know not what they do." They are doing the best they can with what they know; they just don't know enough.

Being offended is a waste of time and energy. I choose to see situations and people accurately. I choose to let go of all judgment, resentment, and hate. I understand that I get what I give. If I choose a mindset of condemning others, I am choosing it for myself, too, and I will always feel judged, unsafe, and not good enough. This is not how I want to live. I choose to give love, forgiveness, and innocence to all so I can live in peace, feeling good enough all the time.

This is my official policy and procedure when I am mistreated:

When someone offends or hurts me, I use the Forgiveness Formula to process my way to Clarity. I get out some paper and answer the questions before I react.

It is my policy to run through the Forgiveness Formula or the Clarity Formula in my head in each situation to be sure I am seeing myself, the other person, and the situation accurately.

I remember that I am here to learn and love – my number one purpose for being here is to learn how to forgive myself and others. This situation is in my life to serve that process. I choose to respond with love.

Write some new policies about how you will handle mistreatment from now on. Because mistreatment happens almost daily, it is important to have clearly defined policies in place ahead of time. Include the Forgiveness Formula as one of your official procedures.

17 – Forgiving Yourself

We all make mistakes (on occasion) and experience some guilt or shame. Guilt and shame are especially painful because they trigger your biggest core fear – *the fear of not being good enough.* Every time you make a mistake this fear flares up and beats you down. The good news is that you can create some healthy policies ahead of time about making mistakes and how you will process these experiences, and doing this will really help.

Guilt and shame are necessary parts of the human experience, though. They teach you important lessons about life and who you don't want to be. They also give you compassion and empathy for other people and make you a lot less judgmental. But there is nothing about guilt and shame that serves you in the long term. You are not meant to live in guilt and shame, though some of you live in them all the time; you are generally ashamed of who you are and what you have accomplished, and this is stealing the joy from your life. My hope is that this chapter will put an end to that.

As I wrote earlier, *if your life's purpose is to learn to love, the most important lesson you are here to learn is how to forgive yourself and other people.* The universe will give you lots of opportunities to practice this truth. The better you get at trusting in your infinite value and seeing yourself accurately, the easier forgiveness gets.

When you make mistakes, take a minute to experience the shame and what it feels like. Listen to the interesting things your Voice of Fear has to say about your mistake and your value. When you become conscious of what it says and how you feel, you can then decide what to do with those feelings. You can *embrace them* or *replace them*. Take some time to look for the lesson in the situation and figure out how you will use it to change your future behavior. Then let the shame and guilt go; Holding on to them doesn't serve you in any way; it only keeps you focused on yourself and prevents you from being who you really are. You should not waste *any* time or energy experiencing shame or regret about your past choices. They are done and gone, and they carry no meaning whatsoever about who you are now. They were interesting lessons in your classroom journey. They were locations on your journey. They served a purpose. But they no longer exist, and that purpose is over. *At least you have the option of seeing it that way if you want to* – or you can keep wallowing in shame. It's up to you.

clarity**point**: **Guilt and shame are fear-based emotions. They are also choices.** You don't have to dwell in them; you can choose to experience situations in trust and love instead.

Some people appear to like shame. Some believe shame is a good thing because it can help you see what you need to change and be a catalyst for change. The problem is that shame isn't all that motivating. Many who suffer with guilt and shame (especially religiously motivated shame) eventually give up. They are convinced they will never measure up in the end, so why try? *Knowing you are loved and infinitely valuable is a lot more motivating.*

I recently made a mistake I felt really badly about. It wasn't anything big, but it bothers me when I'm anything less than perfect because I have that old policy in my head that says *"You have to be perfect or they won't love you."* Consciously I know this isn't true, but my subconscious mind and the Voice of Fear still believe it. When I made the mistake I experienced some shame about it. At first I took a minute to experience those feelings. I walked into the shame and tried it on. I sat with those feelings awhile and really embraced the fear of failure they were encouraging.

Then I decided that living there long term wouldn't serve me or the person I'd offended. Instead I decided to change my mind about the whole thing. I thanked the shame for showing up in my life and reminding me who I want to be. I embraced the beautiful lesson the mistake had taught me and committed to behaving differently in the future. I also apologized to the person I'd hurt. Then I let the experience go. I wiped it out of my mind forever and gone. It was no longer important nor did it mean anything about who I am. This is the best way to handle mistake situations.

We naturally want to do good and be good. We don't need a lot of guilt or shame to motivate us to work on ourselves and improve; we already want that. Trusting that your value is infinite and absolute is more motivating and encouraging than guilt or shame. *Seeing yourself as good makes you want to improve more than seeing yourself as bad does.* But you get to decide how you want to experience your mistakes. You can continue to think guilt and shame are beneficial if you want to, but know that there is another option.

Tom's Story

Tom had made a big mistake and was really upset when he called me. Not only had he been caught, but everyone in his small town knew about his mistake, and he was completely humiliated. For the next few months he endured looks and whispers of judgment from everyone he knew. His friends disappeared and even his family withdrew their support. He felt worthless. The guilt and shame were eating him alive.

The first thing I did was help Tom understand who he really was. He had seen himself as a good person the day before he made the mistake, but the day after his Voice of Fear convinced him he was a terrible, evil person. Through some coaching he began to understand that one mistake, even a really BIG one, didn't change who he was. At his core he was still the same good person. He had made a bad choice, but he was not bad.

I helped Tom create some new personal policies about his real value being infinite and absolute, with which he replaced his negative, fear-based thoughts about his value. This was difficult at first, but he kept at it and refused to allow guilt and shame to take over.

Tom quickly recognized that he had the power to choose how to feel about himself every day. He decided to trust that God loved him in spite of the mistake. He chose to believe that he was still worthy of love and blessings. He decided to see himself as a good person in spite of one bad choice. It was only his Voice of Fear that wanted him to think otherwise.

He also realized that when he was dwelling in guilt and shame he felt disconnected from other people. These negative feelings prevented him from expressing love for others. He realized that nothing he felt while absorbed in guilt and shame was the truth. This experience helped him understand how his Voice of Fear worked. He started to recognize its voice and tell it to shut up. He started choosing trust-and-love-based thoughts instead.

During this time Tom did not want to be around people. He wanted to hide and never come out. But he came to accept that this behavior wouldn't serve anyone. So he decided to see himself instead as a good man who had the strength to make it through the situation and make some changes in his life. He held his head high and went back to work, determined to be the good, kind person he knew he was. He ignored the negative comments from his co-workers and focused all his energy on being kind and respectful. He looked for opportunities to edify and validate the people around him. This was a challenge because they weren't being very nice, but he did it anyway. He soon discovered that even though his mistake had been a big one, it did not define him. He was still a good person.

Tom learned some important lessons from this experience that helped him figure out what kind of man he really wanted to be. He dedicated himself to being the best father and friend possible. It did not take long for the people in his town and his family to change their opinions of him. They could tell that he had a good heart, and because he chose to reach out in kindness, they forgave him.

But as you can imagine, Tom's Voice of Fear continued to encourage guilt. He had to make a policy against guilt and shame thoughts. He made it against his rules to let his thoughts go there. He learned to replace every negative thought that showed up with one based in trust and love. He used the Clarity Formula to see himself and his situation accurately. He claimed the power of conscious choice to decide how he would experience the mistake, and it made all the difference.

When you make mistakes, especially big ones, you will experience some guilt and shame. These are natural responses to bad choices. The question is what are you going to do with those feelings?

Your Voice of Fear will encourage you to dwell in the shame and hold the mistake against your value. It will tell you that you should have known better and that you are worthless because you didn't. Don't listen to it. Give yourself permission to be a work in progress.

* *

clarity**point**: **S.H.A.M.E. is an acronym that stands for Should Have Already Mastered Everything**. This is ridiculous. You are a student in the classroom of life. You are still learning and growing. Give yourself permission to be a work in progress.

* *

The Voice of Fear in your head will try to convince you that your mistakes determine your value. It wants you to wallow in self-pity about what a failure you have been in the past. This fear-based drama can drag on for years, if not decades. Past mistakes can completely devastate your future if you let them. Don't let them. Remember that your value is infinite and absolute no matter what you do. Mistakes can't change who you are or your value.

Take the time to create a personal policy about quickly forgiving yourself for mistakes. Remember that mistakes are part of the learning process, and you are expected to make some – lots, actually. Remember that life on this planet is no cakewalk either. Don't kid yourself into thinking you *"should have known better"* and should not have made a wrong choice.

You had to learn that lesson through the mistake. You were not meant to have it all figured out back then. You had to go through it to learn what it taught you, and you are going to make more mistakes moving forward. You will do your best, but you are going to have some failures and mess some things up. Get used to the idea.

You are here for the express purpose of having terrifying, humiliating, interesting, embarrassing, and even heart-breaking human experiences – so that you can learn from them. You are not meant to fly through this journey with perfect grades. Your mistakes help you fully understand life, people, and yourself. They help you decide what kind of person you want to be. They make you more compassionate and nonjudgmental of others. *They serve you.* But they have nothing to do with your value because your value isn't on the line.

My Personal Policy and Procedure about Making Mistakes

This is my official policy about making mistakes:

> *It is my official policy that mistakes don't affect my value. They are lessons or locations on my journey through life. They do not define who I am. I give myself permission to be a work in progress and a student in the classroom of life. When I make mistakes I embrace the lesson, commit to do better in the future, and let go of guilt and shame. My value is infinite and absolute, and I am*

right on track in my personal process of growth. A mistake does not change that. I often reread this policy when I feel guilt and shame to help me change my thinking.

This is my official procedure for forgiving myself when I make a mistake:

I can change the way I think and feel about mistakes. I have the power to choose how I want to experience them. I choose to use the Clarity Formula to be sure I am in trust and seeing myself and other people accurately. This formula helps me see myself as the same as other people. We are all struggling, scared, divine, amazing beings in process. I do not see myself as less than anyone else. Everyone makes mistakes. We are all the same.

I choose to trust that my value isn't on the line and that I have the same value no matter how many mistakes I make. I remember that S.H.A.M.E. stands for Should Have Already Mastered Everything. This is ridiculous. I am in class, and I always have more to learn. I don't expect myself to be perfect all the time and I don't expect others to be, either. I choose to see myself and others accurately and with love and compassion. I quickly apologize and make amends when I can. Then I commit to doing better in the future. After that I let the mistake slip into the past without any effect on my future or my value. It was just a lesson.

This is your chance to write some new official policies about how you will process and experience your bad choices. You can wallow in shame and guilt if you'd like, or you can choose a mindset of trust and love.

Make it your policy to avoid bad choices as often as possible so you can create the best quality life you can, but keep occasional mistakes in proper perspective and process them in Clarity.

18 – Dealing with Difficult People

Every person who shows up in your life is there to teach you something, and most are here to help you learn to love and forgive at a deeper level. Most of these people will teach you forgiveness by pushing your buttons, annoying you, aggravating you, or making you crazy, thereby giving you the opportunity to practice choosing love over fear. *Isn't that nice of them?*

Some of the people in your world are specifically there to show you the limits of your love (a term Marianne Williamson coined in her book *A Return to Love*). You need to know your limits so you know where to work. These people show you where you need to work on yourself by mirroring back your own fear and bad behavior. Let me give you an example. I am really bothered by people who judge other people. It bothers me when I see someone being judged or rejected. You can see why this is a perfect lesson for me. *I am doing the very thing I am bothered by them for doing.* They are serving as a mirror for me so I can see where I need more love.

If you choose to, you can experience the difficult people in your life as teachers and have curiosity and gratitude for the lessons they are teaching you. It's not always easy to see them this way and be grateful for them, but it's a good idea because it's accurate.

. . . .

clarity**point**: **Difficult people are the teachers in your life. They are here to provide opportunities to grow, learn, forgive, and love.**

. . . .

When faced with difficult people, you must remember that your value is not on the line. Nothing they do or say can diminish you in any way. Even if they attack you, criticize you, or wrongfully accuse you, you can stay calm and unaffected, knowing you are bulletproof, if you want to. You have the same infinite value no matter what they do or think.

You have the power to choose how you are going to react to these people and situations. No one can *make* you angry or *make* you feel badly about yourself; you choose to be angry and you choose to feel badly. *You are in control of your thoughts and how you feel.* But if you don't consciously choose your response and attitude, your subconscious mind will choose for you; and it will usually choose fear.

. . . .

clarity**point**: **No one has the power to hurt or diminish you unless you give them that power.** Your value is infinite and absolute. You are bulletproof.

. . . .

If you have been letting your subconscious policies drive your reactions to difficult people most of your life, it might feel like you can't control your emotions; but that's a cop-out, because you can. You have the power to choose how you want to experience everything that happens.

When dealing with a difficult person, the first thing you must do is run through the Clarity Formula in your head. You must make sure you see yourself accurately as a divine, amazing, struggling, scared student in the classroom of life. Remember that your value is not on the line because life is a classroom, not a test. There is nothing this person can do that will diminish you. This neutralizes your first core fear – *the fear that you aren't good enough.* Then remember that your life is the perfect classroom journey for you. Your experience with this person is in your life to teach you something. This neutralizes your second core fear – *the fear of loss or that your life isn't good enough.*

Now make sure you are seeing the other person accurately and choose to see them as the same as you – a divine, amazing, struggling, scared student in the classroom of life who is doing the best they can with what they know. You might ask yourself, "What is this person afraid of?" and "What do they need in this moment?" If you can answer these two questions, you will understand what is really motivating their behavior. You might even want to directly ask them questions about how they feel or think so you will know for sure what's going on in their head.

....

clarity**point**: **Fear is the root cause of most bad behavior.**
When others behave badly, it is not about you;
it is about their fear of not being good enough
or their fear of loss.

....

Here is another truth about human behavior that can
help you understand others:

....

clarity**point**: **People who behave badly want you to
behave badly, too, because it takes the
focus off their bad behavior.** They push your
buttons and try to drag you into fear with them.

....

People functioning in fear desperately want to drag you
into fear and bad behavior with them. They subconsciously
think that getting you to behave badly back somehow excuses
their bad behavior and shifts the focus to how bad you are.
Don't fall for this. Stay calm, bulletproof, and respectful no
matter how out of control they get. This will force them to
own their bad behavior.

....

clarity**point**: **If you can stay in trust and love, it takes
all the fun out of others' attacks and forces
them to own their bad behavior.**

....

When others are in fear and behaving badly, don't take anything they say personally. Remember that their anger and frustration is not about you. Their problem is always about their fears about themselves. *Their attack is about how they feel about themselves.* It is a sign of their self-hate. This is a universal truth and it means all bad behavior is really a request for love, attention, or validation. This person is afraid and needs validation to quiet their fear. You must step back from every mistreatment situation and see this. If you don't see the situation accurately you will react badly.

* *

clarity**point**: **All bad behavior is really a request for love, attention, or validation.**

* *

The worse a person's behavior is, the greater their need for love, attention, or validation, though their bad behavior will not make you want to love or validate them. If you can set aside your ego and the need to be right, and give them what they need even though they might not deserve it, you will feel amazing and powerful. Choosing love in these moments feels incredible.

You can use the Clarity Questions below to make sure you are seeing any situation accurately and responding appropriately. These questions will help you stay in trust and love and find the most appropriate and loving response. You might want to mark this page so you can come back to it often.

(You can download a Clarity Questions Worksheet at my website, www.claritypointcoaching.com.)

The Clarity Questions

1. Do I remember that my value is infinite and absolute, that no one can diminish me, and that I am the same me no matter what they do or say?

2. Do I remember that my life is the perfect classroom journey for me and that every experience is a lesson?

3. Do I see this person as the same as me? Can I see that they are a work in progress, just like me?

4. Can I see what they are afraid of? Are they afraid of loss or afraid they aren't good enough?

5. What do they need right now?

6. Are they tired, hungry, or incapable of mature behavior because they haven't had the opportunity to learn it? What has happened in their life that affects their current behavior?

7. What are some possible options in response to this situation? (See how many options you can come up with. This is an exercise in being solution-focused rather than problem-focused.)

8. Next to each option you identified in question 7, write down what you think the outcome of that option would be. How will people react if you respond that way? What results will that choice create?

9. Now look at each option from question 7 and cross out the fear-based responses. Choose an option with a Clarity-based response that feels right to you.

This process helps you see the other person accurately and understand the real reason they are being so difficult. It helps you find compassion for their situation and see the fear that is driving their bad behavior. In most situations you will find yourself with these two wise and loving options:

1. Forgive them for being afraid, confused, and angry (mostly at themselves), and let their bad behavior go. Just forgive it because you understand that we are all students in the classroom of life and have a lot to learn. Decide to give them room to be imperfect and growing. Let the offense go, never to think of it again.

2. Use the Communication Formula and have a mutually validating conversation about the situation. Validate them and listen to how they feel. Then ask permission to share how you feel and ask them if they would be willing to change their behavior moving forward.

Either of these two options would work and help you handle this person from trust and love. As you step it up and choose to become more aware, accurate, and loving, your relationships will greatly improve... not because the other person has changed but because you have.

When you make this change it might cause a fundamental shift in the people around you, too. They cannot treat you or respond to you the way they did before. When you no longer bring fear into the relationship, the entire relationship changes.

Cheri's Story

Cheri had been criticized and put down by her stepfather her whole life. He took every opportunity to make her feel small and stupid. Cheri was in her fifties when she came to me for coaching, and her stepfather was still causing her a great deal of pain. She often went to visit her mother but would usually cut the visits short after her stepfather criticized her into tears.

She called me after one of these terrible visits and I was blown away by the self-pity and fear that engulfed her. This man was able to completely destroy her self-esteem in less than an hour. Cheri was a beautiful, smart, capable lady with a successful career, but she let this toxic person reduce her to nothing. She had to stop being afraid of him and remember the truth about her value.

I helped Cheri realize that her stepfather's opinion of her was irrelevant; it didn't affect her value or diminish her. She was the same smart, good, successful person regardless of what he thought. She had nothing to be afraid of because his words and opinions didn't mean anything. They couldn't hurt her unless she chose to let them hurt her. She needed to step back and see the situation accurately.

I also encouraged her to have some compassion for him. He was a sad, scared, miserable person who had serious self-esteem and anger issues. As she began to see the situation more accurately, without her fear of not being good enough skewing her perspective, she started to feel compassion for him instead of anger. This was a step in the right direction.

Next we worked on Cheri's self-esteem. I helped her discover her Voice of Truth, and she started to see herself as a beautiful, loving, compassionate, strong woman. She recognized the great love she had for other people and started to reach out to others more often and look for opportunities to validate everyone she met. After some time went by she started to visualize herself interacting with her stepfather and having compassion for and patience with him. She saw herself smiling and letting his insults bounce off. She saw herself being calm and kind in spite of anything he did. She practiced, through visualization, feeling bulletproof no matter what he said.

Over the next month a change occurred in Cheri that was so dramatic that she almost became a different person.

Every fear she had been carrying with her for her whole life was being replaced with love. She was no longer scared about anything. She was full of love for herself and for other people. She started excelling in her career, meeting people, and making new friends. Everything in her life was changing. It was time to visit her stepfather.

She took a minute before going into the house to remind herself of her value and who she was. Then she went inside with her head held high. It was not an ego attitude, though; Cheri was filled with trust and love. She was fearless, kind, and loving towards both of her parents. She asked lots of questions and tried to edify them. The visit went exactly as she had envisioned except for one big difference – her stepfather was kinder. He wasn't as rude as he had been in the past.

I explained to her later that when you are filled with fear, people around you subconsciously sense it, and they are more likely to victimize you. Your fearful energy invites them to mistreat you. Your energy says, "I'm a victim; take from me," so they do. When you consistently show up in fear, people lose respect for you, and this is what had happened with her stepfather.

Now Cheri wasn't scared anymore. She was fearless and loving. Now her energy was strong, not weak. When you show up this way, people can feel that, too. They can feel your strength and confidence, and they will treat you with more respect. Now that she was showing up with strength and love, she was someone her stepfather could respect.

The best way to deal with difficult people is to be so balanced in trust and love that they just don't bother you. Feeling strong, wise, and bulletproof is not difficult, but it will require some practice, especially if you have let your fear-based emotions run the show for a long time. But the more you work at it, the easier it becomes.

If you practice using the Clarity Questions to process situations in your life accurately, your subconscious mind will eventually get with the system, and this healthy process will become your new autopilot. You must also listen to your Voice of Truth in each specific situation. You are entitled to guidance from your Voice-of-Truth side to help you find the right response in each situation; just pay attention to it and trust that the answer will be there.

My Personal Policies about Dealing with Difficult People

This is my official policy about human behavior and seeing other people and their behavior accurately:

> I understand that difficult people are in my life to help me grow. They often mistreat me or offend me. When this happens, I remember that my value isn't on the line and I cannot be diminished. This prevents me from giving them the power to hurt me.
>
> I also remember that most bad behavior isn't about me; it is about their fears about themselves. All bad behavior is a request for love, attention, or validation. If I can stay in trust and love, it

can take the fear out of the situation. I use the Clarity Formula to help me stay in trust and love.

I have compassion for miserable people and it is my official policy not to take anything they do or say personally. That doesn't mean that I let them walk on me, though. I speak my trust and defend my boundaries, but I do it with love.

This is my official policy about handling difficult situations appropriately:

I believe that love is the highest law there is. I choose to handle every situation with love. Even if I forget this in the moment and react in fear, I quickly shift gears and use the Clarity Questions to help me choose trust and love. I use the Clarity Questions Worksheet to find the most appropriate and loving solution to every problem.

Create a new policy about using the Clarity Questions to handle difficult situations, and read through your policies daily for a while. Using your notebook will help you keep all your policies and procedures together so you can review them easily.

19 – Love Motivation

Changing your old subconscious policies and adopting new trust-and-loved-based policies will take some time and practice. Don't expect to master this new way of thinking overnight. I've been teaching these principles for years, and it has become easier and easier to reign in my fear, but it's still a battle. The Voice of Fear is not going anywhere. It will continue to drag you into fear every moment you are alive. It will beat you up for every mistake and constantly tell you that you aren't good enough. I want you to see this coming, especially if you have issues with perfectionism.

Every time you learn a new skill, the Voice of Fear will tell you that you have to be perfect at it. And if you aren't perfect at it, which you can't be since you are just learning, the Voice of Fear will use your imperfectness to make you feel like you aren't good enough all over again. You might already be experiencing this when it comes to what you have learned in *Choosing Clarity*. You might already feel inadequate in your effort to choose trust and love. To battle this, you must make sure your expectations are realistic. If your expectations are too high, you will always feel like a failure.

Remember that the Voice of Fear in your head has an agenda. It uses perfectionistic standards on purpose to keep you in fear so you will be too distracted to love other people. It wants you to be so focused on proving your value and being perfect that you literally can't show up for others. So the Voice of Fear judges your performance (and everything you do) on a scale of "it's perfect" or "it's not good enough," with nothing in between. It literally says you have to be perfect to have value. This is not true, of course. You have infinite and absolute value no matter how you perform.

Having said that, you will always feel better about yourself when you set goals, work hard, achieve results, and do your best. Trusting in your infinite value does not mean being so content that you stop stretching. It does not mean getting apathetic and comfortable where you are. It means setting goals, working hard, and achieving results *while being in trust about your value the whole time.* It means that no matter what results you create at the end, your value is still the same. It means you are not scared of not being good enough because you understand that isn't possible.

You might have worried about this as you read this book. You might have had some fear about lowering your expectations and letting go of the fear that has been driving your efforts. You might have been afraid that it would make you lose motivation to work hard. *You might think that motivation requires fear.* I understand this, especially if fear motivation is what you grew up with and all you have known. But it's just not true.

clarity**point**: **Love is more motivating than fear.**

Love motivation works better. But if you have spent your entire life being fear-motivated, you might have no idea what love motivation even looks like.

Let me introduce you to the concept: Love motivation is about being motivated by passion and joy. It is based on your love for God, life, yourself, and other people. It is about building, creating, and working to achieve great things because of the wonderful results they create in your life, not because you need that achievement to prove you are good enough. Love motivation means doing things out of passion because you want to, not because you should or have to. In this place, you are still motivated to work hard and achieve great things, but you have no fear about making mistakes or failing because failing isn't possible. With love motivation, your value is not attached to your results, so no matter what happens it is your perfect next lesson. *When your value isn't on the line you are still motivated to work hard and create the life you want, but you know you are safe in the process.*

Motivation does not require stress and fear. It just requires a *why*. As long as you have a good reason to do something you will be motivated to do it, and love is a very powerful why. Think about the last time you did something you love doing. That was love motivation at work. Love motivation is a joyful experience. If you look closely you will see that the most successful people on this planet are motivated by love, not fear. They have a passion for what they do and that passion drives them to success. You can live this way, too.

clarity**point**: **You can live in joy and passion, driven by love for God, yourself, others, and life; or you can choose to be motivated by fear of failure or fear of losing what you have. You get to choose how to live.**

The motivation or the why behind what you do matters because it determines the energy you bring to the situation. If you volunteer to take charge of a project at work because you are afraid people will think less of you if you don't, it feels very different than if you volunteer because you love the chance to stretch yourself and try new things, or you love the company and want to serve, or you love your family and want to excel to provide for them. Those are love-motivated whys.

If you babysit your neighbor's kid because you feel too guilty to say no, you will probably hate every minute of it and resent the neighbor for asking you to. This is a fear-motivated experience that will only perpetuate fear and resentment.

If you start jogging to lose some weight so people will approve of you, this is a fear-motivated experience based in your fear of not being good enough. Instead, you might want to choose a form of exercise that you love to do and makes you happy. This makes exercise a love-motivated experience. Or you could choose to see exercise as a way to become healthy because you love feeling good, rather than because you want to look a certain way to earn approval from others.

Think about some of the things you do and ask yourself why you do them. *Do you have a love-motivated reason or a fear-motivated reason?* If you are motivated by fear, stop doing it, do something different, or change your attitude. Choose to do things only for love-motivated reasons.

You get to decide in each moment how you want to experience your life, and remember this is a simple choice because there are only two options. If you find yourself having a fear-motivated experience, you can change your attitude in an instant and find a love-motivated reason to do what you are doing. Make it your official policy to live from passion and love.

My Personal Policies about Perfectionism and Motivation

This is my official policy about perfectionism:

> *I have a terrible subconscious core fear that I have to be perfect or no one will love me. This is something I have to be very aware of and watch for. Because of this strong subconscious fear, it is my official policy not to even try to do anything perfectly. I know that perfection is not possible, and I do not put pressure on myself to achieve it. I continue to grow, learn, and do my best every day, but I don't beat myself up for mistakes.*

I have an official policy not to compare myself with other people. It is against my rules. They are signed up for totally different classes, and I am on a personal journey of growth made just for me. I choose to focus more on loving other people than on proving my value, because my value is not in question.

This is my official policy about motivation and why I do what I do:

Every day, in everything I do, I choose to be love motivated.

I live life in joy and love for God, life, other people, myself, learning, and growing. I have a passion for working hard and creating results because I want to fill the measure of my creation and become the best I can be. When I make mistakes, I ask myself what I can learn from them and how I can improve next time.

Failing isn't on the table. Failing isn't possible when there is no test; every experience is a beautiful lesson. I choose to live in trust and love.

Deciding to live your life with passion and joy is a choice you get to make. It is in your power. Write some new personal policies about living in passion and joy and joy in your notebook.

20 – Embracing Life

Throughout *Choosing Clarity* we have talked about escaping fear and trusting the process of life. But let's be honest; it is not that easy because life is a scary and dangerous place, and bad things happen all the time. If you are going to be able to escape fear successfully, it is critical you understand how your brain is subconsciously programmed to respond to scary situations.

You are programmed with an automatic *fight or flight* response that kicks in whenever you are scared. It has to be this way so you don't waste time thinking about what to do when your life is in danger. This is a subconscious policy that serves you when you are faced with physical danger.

Imagine walking down the street and all of a sudden a hungry alligator charges out of the bushes straight towards you. You react automatically. Your body is flooded with adrenaline and some parts of your brain shut down so the rest can respond to the threat. Which would you unconsciously choose first – *to run* or *to fight* the alligator? Think about it for a minute.

Most likely you chose to run because running and escaping is the option less likely to end with pain and blood loss. If running or avoiding a scary thing is an option, you will always subconsciously choose that option first. If you get cornered and cannot run, you would choose to fight; but you are subconsciously programmed to avoid scary and painful things if possible.

The *flight* reaction makes sense when you are faced with a hungry alligator, but it does not make sense when you are faced with other scary things like financial problems, a breakup, losing your job, not having friends, or problems with your spouse or children. *You cannot run from these kinds of situations; you must fight your way through.* But your subconscious mind doesn't want to fight. It will try to ignore or hide from these problems for as long as it can.

Are you running from something scary in your life right now? Are you hiding your head in the sand hoping the problem will go away on its own? Are you procrastinating about dealing with it? Do you distract yourself with hobbies or work because you don't know how to fix it? Do you leave mail unopened because you don't want to see the bills? Are you avoiding taking on your life and solving your problems?

This behavior is not worthy of who you are. It also defies your purpose for being here (to learn and grow) when you run, hide, or procrastinate in dealing with life. Your Voice of Fear thinks it is protecting you with these avoidance tactics, but it is really thwarting your growth and preventing you from becoming who you are meant to be.

clarity**point**: **When you avoid problems or procrastinate about fixing them, they don't go away; they get bigger.**

You might not consciously realize you are hiding, though. Your subconscious mind might be using clever distractions to keep your mind off solving your problems. It is important that you wake up and become consciously aware of this self-sabotage. Do you employ any of these common ways to avoid what you're scared of?:

- Do you watch a lot of TV?
- Do you watch a lot of movies?
- Do you read a lot of books?
- Do you view pornography or indulge in romance novels to experience pleasure that you can't find in the real world?
- Do you spend time on get-rich-quick business ideas? Do you look for shortcuts to a fantasy life?
- Do you spend money you don't have without considering your financial reality?
- Do you use drugs or alcohol?
- Do you focus on work or hobbies while ignoring other areas of your life? Do you spend time on them instead of doing things that would improve your current situation?
- Do you pretend that everything is fine in your relationships when it's not?

- Do you struggle with procrastination? Do you procrastinate about the very activities that could change your life for the better?

Take an honest inventory of your behavior. Do you use any of these things to kill the pain you are currently experiencing? Do you feel happy only when you are distracted from your life?

If you waste too much time doing any of these things, you are literally *wasting your life* and ignoring your purpose. You are meant to embrace living and take on challenges. You are meant to work things out, solve problems, stretch, and grow. You are here to learn how to create good relationships and connect with other people. *It is time to take responsibility for your life and start living it!*

Decide today to be more responsible for your life and to stop running. Recognize the excuses you have used in the past and drop them. Do any of these excuses sound familiar?

- I'm too busy.
- I have too much on my plate.
- I can't do more.
- I never learned how to deal with these things.
- There's nothing I can do.
- I wasn't given the right opportunities.
- I'm not smart enough.
- I don't have enough money.
- I have no support.

Own the excuses you are using to avoid learning and growing. This behavior is not worthy of you. You can do better. You are meant to be better. Embrace your scary challenges, ask for help, learn some new skills, and fight your way through. The only thing in your way is fear. Fear of failure, rejection, being embarrassed, or looking bad is what makes you avoid trying new things, talking to new people, and solving problems. But if you live like this, you aren't really living. *A boat is safe in the harbor, but that is not what boats are meant for.*

Don't sacrifice living to protect yourself from being embarrassed. Ask for help; it doesn't mean you are weak, it means you are smart. Trust that what other people think of you doesn't matter. Their opinions don't change anything; you are the same you no matter how many embarrassing failures you experience or who sees them. *Your value is infinite and absolute no matter what.* If you decide to see failures accurately, as nothing more than lessons, you can start living again.

- -

clarity**point**:   **What other people think doesn't change who you are. You are the same you no matter what.**

- -

Perhaps you suffer from a fear of success, which means you're afraid of the responsibilities and commitments that come with raising the bar and shooting higher; you might actually feel safer shooting low and setting goals that are easy to reach so you are less at risk. But if do this, you will never find out who you really are. *You are capable of much more than you think, and there is nothing to fear!*

That is the whole point of this book.

• •

clarity**point: There is really nothing to fear.**

• •

There is nothing to fear about shooting high and taking risks because you cannot fail or be not good enough – you can only learn. Besides, you don't have to be ready to carry the responsibilities of the end goal at the beginning. Learning and growth happen slowly, step by step. By the time you get to the highest level, you will be ready for it. Stop letting F.E.A.R. (False Evidence Appearing Real) stop you.

Use the Clarity Formula to escape your fear in any situation. It really works. Run through the steps in your head to see situations accurately and feel capable, confident, and strong. You won't need to make excuses and you won't waste time with unnecessary drama and procrastination. *Clarity is a no-drama and no-excuses zone.* When you choose to live in Clarity, you can take more risks, shoulder more responsibility, and shoot higher. You can live with passion and joy. You can become the person you are meant to be, and it's easier than you think.

Evan's Story

Evan was completely overwhelmed all the time. He had so much on his plate that he couldn't get to the important projects he needed to do. Every week in coaching he complained about his life and how busy he was. Every week he became more discouraged because again and again, he never started those important projects.

I gave Evan some time-management tips and suggested ways he might fit the important projects into his week, but it never happened. I started to suspect that there was a deeper problem and that Evan's subconscious mind was sabotaging him. As I asked more questions, we uncovered some serious fear-of-failure issues regarding these projects. He was afraid he wouldn't do them well enough, and he really didn't want to be responsible for the outcomes. His subconscious mind was using "being overwhelmed" as an excuse to get out of taking responsibility for the projects.

The truth was that he wasn't all that busy; he just filled his days with a hundred little unimportant tasks that made him feel busy and productive even though he wasn't. He created a story of being overwhelmed by all these unimportant tasks so he could feel too busy to take on anything else. *He used being overwhelmed to hide from his responsibilities.* By complaining constantly about the giant load he was carrying, he felt justified in avoiding the projects.

I taught Evan the Clarity Formula so he could escape his fears and take on his life. He decided to trust that his value would not be affected by the outcome of the projects. He chose to trust that his journey was the perfect journey for him, to believe that the projects would unfold exactly as they were meant to, and that he would be okay no matter what happened. He also learned to consciously recognize the urgings of his Voice of Fear that wanted him to avoid the projects. He chose to ignore it and scheduled time to do the projects, even though he was afraid. Once he started working, an amazing thing happened; he realized he loved the work. He found joy in the projects and felt passionate about finishing them. The fear disappeared.

Writing some official policies about taking on life will make a huge difference in how you handle challenges. Here is my personal policy:

My Personal Policy about Embracing Life

I understand that my subconscious mind is programmed to avoid scary things. It is my official policy not to let this happen.

I consciously watch for procrastination and fear regarding the challenges in my life. I am meant to take on these challenges and solve them. I was born to win, not fail. The great truth that helps me is "there is nothing to fear"; this life is a perfect classroom experience made just for me. I am safe in this process.

When I am faced with a problem it is my policy to ask for help, embrace the challenge, and trust that God will help me win. I brainstorm possible solutions and stay solution-focused, not problem-focused. I choose to stay positive and hopeful about everything in my life. Good things happen to me.

Now it's your turn to practice being more responsible. Own the challenges you have been avoiding and stop hiding from your life. Ask for help, brainstorm possible solutions, and trust that the answers you need will be there. Create a new policy about taking on challenges even though they scare you.

21 – Relationship Rules

The quality of your life is largely dependent on the quality of your relationships. This is especially true of your relationship will your significant other. This relationship will provide the best moments, the worst moments, and the best lessons of your life. This important person is going to teach you, stretch you, test you, try you, and sometimes rip you apart, all in an effort to show you your fears and give you the chance to grow. I know this because you are here in the classroom of life to learn, and that is the point of everything.

The universe knows exactly what kinds of challenges you need to become the person you are meant to be. So you will always be attracted to the person who is your best possible teacher. This means you are in each other's lives to teach each other, and especially to teach each other about love, compassion, and forgiveness.

clarity**point**: **Your significant other provides the most important lessons in your life.** The purpose of life is to learn, and this person is your greatest teacher.

This means the conflict, fighting, or resentment showing up in your relationship right now is there for a reason. It is there to show you things about yourself and give you the opportunity to improve yourself. It is not there just to drive you crazy. *Your life is the perfect classroom journey for you, and there are no accidents.* So every problem that shows up in your relationship has a purpose behind it.

It has been fascinating over the years to see that every couple I meet with has the perfect storm when it comes to their core fears *in that they perfectly trigger each other.* The bad behavior created by his core fear perfectly triggers her core fear, and the bad behavior her core fear creates perfectly triggers his core fear. This creates an amazing (yet very challenging) environment for learning.

Your job in your relationship is to work on your own fears and learn how to escape them so you can become more loving. But everyone's journey is unique. Some relationships are in your life to give you the opportunity to become strong and summon the strength to leave. Other relationships are there because you are meant to fix the problems, escape fear, and become a better person. Only you know the right answer for you in your specific situation. Having said that, I believe most relationship problems are fixable.

If you want to change your relationship for the better, you must start by getting your fear under control. *The solution always lies in changing you and escaping fear.* Even if you think your partner is the one with the problems, it is never a one way street. The conflict and suffering in your relationship could not survive without your participation at some level.

claritypoint: You have both made mistakes and treated each other unkindly. (It doesn't matter who was bad first or who was worse.) **The only way to fix your relationship is for each of you to fix your own fear-based behavior.**

Both of you should commit to changing the relationship, but even if you are the only one willing to work on it, your changing you can sometimes be enough. When you make fundamental changes in your attitude and show up without fear, it changes the energy you bring to the relationship, which changes the way the other person feels about you. If you show up with trust and love, the fear (that was the root of your problems to begin with) dissipates and the dynamics of the relationship change – because they have to; they cannot stay the same.

This shift either fixes the relationship or makes it obvious that you don't belong together. *But you should not make this determination until you are in Clarity and out of fear.* Fear skews your perspective.

clarity**point**: **When one person changes, the energy in the relationship changes, and the other person cannot behave the same way.** A change in you always causes a change in them.

In the end you cannot totally fix any relationship by yourself, though. Your partner is responsible for their part of the problem, and at some point they will need to change their behavior. But you can be the catalyst to get the process of change started.

clarity**point**: **If you insist on waiting for your significant other to change first, they will feel the same way and you will both wait forever. Be the one to choose love over fear first.**

The secret to changing your relationship lies in each person working on their own self-esteem. Almost all relationship problems are based in self-esteem problems, *driven by your core fear of not being good enough.* When you experience this fear on a daily basis (which most of us do), you can become selfish, protective, defensive, and incapable of showing up for the other person. You aren't capable of love if you are in fear. In many relationships both partners are suffering with self-esteem issues and both are primarily focused on getting the love they need, which means *no one is giving any.* This is a recipe for disaster.

To fix this, you must start seeing yourself and your value accurately. Remember that no one can diminish you or disvalue you in any way. Your value is infinite and absolute and does not require validation from your partner. You have the same value no matter what your partner says or does. When you fully grasp this concept, you will be more capable of showing love to your partner because you won't need anything from them. You will release them from being responsible for your self-esteem.

clarity**point**: **Your partner is not responsible for making you feel good about yourself; you are responsible for your own self-esteem.** Your sense of worth comes from the principles of truth you adopt.

Nothing your partner says or does can fix your fear of not being good enough. It is a wonderful thing if you have a partner who validates you, but you should never depend on someone else to fill your empty bucket. They cannot fill it often enough to make up for the fact that you are letting it leak out the other side because you don't see your real value. *They cannot give you self-esteem.* If you continue to expect this person to make you feel loved and worthy, you are setting them up for failure. In the end you will still feel inadequate and you will blame them since you made them responsible for your worth – and this is totally unfair.

You must own responsibility for your self-worth. You must choose to see yourself accurately and love yourself, or nothing your partner does or says will ever be enough to make up for that. Even if they try to validate your worth, you won't believe it. You must believe in your own value first.

In order to have a truly healthy relationship, you must know who you are with rock-solid confidence and you must not allow anyone (or any situation) to take that away from you. You can get this confidence by trusting in your infinite value and your perfect classroom journey *(the two truths from the Clarity Formula)*. You can maintain this confidence by writing strong policies about your worth and reading them often.

If you do not trust in your infinite and absolute value, your fear of not being good enough will poison your relationship. Your insecurity could also cause your partner to lose respect for you. People generally don't respect fear, and fear is not very attractive either.

Confidence is attractive. We are attracted to people who have good self-esteem and know who they are. Your partner might try to love you unconditionally in spite of your low self-esteem, but in the end it will be hard for them to respect you, and you cannot really have love without respect.

I realize this might be hard to hear if you are struggling with low self-esteem, but you need to hear it. You must get committed to an accurate policy about your value and take responsibility for the problems your fear of not being good enough is creating.

clarity**point**: **As long as you doubt your own value, your relationship will suffer.**

If you want to have a good relationship, you must also stop taking your partner's bad behavior personally when it's really about their fears. You must stop creating drama and casting bad guys. The good news is that I've given you all the tools you need in this book to make this happen. Now you just have to practice using them.

Take a minute to think about your past behavior in the relationship. Are you carrying grudges against your partner for offenses in the past? Do you need to work on forgiveness?

If so, use the Forgiveness Formula to get in trust and let it go. Choose not to be offended and recognize that most bad behavior isn't about you to begin with. It is about their fears. Commit to a forgiving mindset and allow your partner room to be a work in progress – just like you.

Be sure you are not applying meaning to events that isn't accurate. Don't apply your core fear to situations in which it doesn't belong. Their bad mood doesn't mean you aren't good enough. Stop making everything they say and feel about you.

Don't create unnecessary drama by keeping score to prove they love you less than you love them. There are no bad guys here. There are only two amazing souls, struggling with their fears and doing the best they can, though sometimes behaving badly. You both do it on occasion, so don't start casting stones.

It is time to grow up, forgive past offenses, and trust that these experiences served you. Stop looking for mistreatment and excuses to justify *your* bad behavior towards your partner. Give your partner permission to make mistakes, lose their cool, and be grouchy on occasion. They are a work in progress, just like you. Honor your partner's classroom journey and give them the space to learn and grow without counting every mistake against them.

Remember that you can only be in one of two places. If you choose fear, you will feel justified in condemning them, but you will also feel terrible about yourself. If you choose trust in your infinite value, and give that gift to them, too, you will feel good about yourself and your relationship with thrive. *How do you want to live?*

The last two steps of the Clarity Formula are especially important in your relationship. You must make sure you are seeing your partner as the same as you. Don't cast your partner as the bad guy, and stop looking for evidence to support your need to be right about your partner not loving you enough. Your partner doesn't love you perfectly because they are battling fear about their own value, which prevents them from being loving. But this has more to do with their fear than your value.

Accept the fact that your partner is an amazing, divine, struggling, scared human being in process, just like you. Give them some room to say and do the wrong things on occasion. Give your partner room to make some mistakes, be less than perfect, and still deserve your love. *That is what love is about – accepting someone who is imperfect, just like you, and loving them anyway.* To do this, you must forgive both your partner and yourself.

. . . .

clarity**point**: **Your ability to forgive your partner determines the quality of your relationship.** If you refuse to let go of past offenses, your relationship won't make it.

. . . .

Perhaps you are holding on to a long list of faults and offenses committed by your partner over the years. You might be very fond of this list because it casts them as the bad guy and you as the innocent victim. You might not want to let go of these offenses because it would feel like letting your partner win. This is an ego problem. You are literally choosing your ego's desire to be better than another person over your happiness. It is time to let go, choose forgiveness, and create a miracle. Here is how one couple did it:

Mark's Story

Mark and his wife had been married for over twenty years, but the spark was gone and there was a lot of resentment built up between them. This was not the kind of relationship Mark wanted, and he had started to fantasize about leaving. I suggested that before he gave up he should give the *Choosing Clarity* approach a try. He was skeptical that anything could change his situation and make him feel better about his marriage. He was also bothered by the idea that he would have to be the one to change, but he agreed it was worth a try.

The first step was to get in trust about his value and his journey. Mark recognized that his resentment came from not feeling validated or appreciated by his wife. She wasn't physically affectionate and this made him feel unwanted and unloved. Her lack of affection triggered his fear of not being good enough. It also triggered his fear of loss, in that he wasn't getting the kind of life he wanted.

I asked him some questions about his self-esteem and he realized he had a huge fear of not being good enough and had suffered with this his whole life. This fear was causing all kinds of problems in the relationship. When he experienced insecurity, he was especially angry about the lack of love and validation in his marriage. He also brought his fear of not being good enough to work. He experienced a lot of stress and fear about his job and he often brought that home with him expecting his wife to take it away. This was not fair. Remember, you can't make your partner responsible for your self-esteem.

Through coaching, Mark owned his part of the problem. He realized that most of the fear in the relationship was coming from him. He realized that if he felt better about himself he might show up differently towards his wife; he might be more capable of giving love, and this might prompt her to give more love back to him.

Mark worked on trusting that his value was infinite and absolute. He worked on being more loving and responding to challenges with more maturity (not casting her as the bad guy). He admitted that he could be kinder and more loving to his wife, and he committed to work on that. He could also be more forgiving and choose more compassion for her struggles. He started to see that his wife was afraid that she wasn't good enough, too, and this fear also held her back from being loving. *Her bad behavior was about her fear, not his value.*

Mark changed the way he experienced the inevitable bumps in their relationship. Instead of seeing everything as an attack, he started to see her behavior more accurately. His wife was afraid she wasn't good enough. Her Voice of Fear told her that everything Mark did or said meant he didn't love her. The main problem in their relationship was that they were both afraid they weren't loved. This meant they were both focused on trying to get the love and validation they needed and no one was giving any.

This situation – with both of them living in fear – had to change. Someone was going to have to set aside their fears and start choosing love, and Mark knew it had to be him. He made a commitment to behave with love even if he didn't get it back. He also worked on being in trust that this relationship was there to help him grow and that the problems could be fixed. He decided to trust the process of life and fight his way through these challenges.

Forgiving his wife for past offenses was really difficult, though. He had become fond of his victim story and how it made him feel. I helped him let go of that story by getting clear about his own offenses. I helped him see that he was also guilty of every offense he held against his wife, so he couldn't cast the first stone. We are all in the same boat fighting the same battle with the same fears. We might react to them in different ways, but no one is better or worse than anyone else. Mark started choosing to see his wife as the same as him. This brought compassion and forgiveness into their relationship.

Forgiveness is much easier when you see your own faults and mistakes and think about how much you'd like to be excused from them. You will create a lot more happiness in your life if you choose a trust-and-love mindset that gives everyone (including you) the right to be flawed, struggling, and scared – and still wonderful, perfect, and good enough – all the time. You will give forgiveness to your partner because you also want it for yourself. If you deny forgiveness and continue to condemn your partner, you won't feel good about yourself either. It's a two-way street. If you chose a judgmental, condemning mindset towards others, it will always affect the way you see yourself. It has to. It is a universal law. Either you chose to see everyone as bad and guilty or you see everyone as infinite and absolute. *How do you want to live?*

Remember that you are not perfect and your partner is not perfect, *but your journey together is perfect.* Your relationship is the perfect classroom for both of you and you are right on track in your personal process of growth. This means you are always good enough, innocent, and valuable.

Mark's Story Continued

Mark decided to forgive his wife and himself for all their past bad behavior and wipe the slate clean every day. This gave him a great deal of peace and confidence to keep doing better. Every morning he let the past go and started over and let her do the same. This made an incredible difference. It wasn't easy, but he could do it.

The last step for Mark was to give more love and validation to his wife. So I taught Mark the Communication Formula. The next day when he came home from work, his wife was sitting at the computer and was obviously frustrated. Usually he would have ignored her, but that day he stopped and asked what she was doing.

She said rather curtly that she was doing everything, as usual, since he didn't do anything to help her anymore. Mark's Voice of Fear encouraged him to say something rude back. It wanted him to get defensive and angry. But he was determined not to go there. That day he chose love. That day he chose to see her bad behavior as a request for love instead of an attack.

He used the Communication Formula to validate her and make her feel important instead of taking it personally and starting a fight. In a kind voice he asked, "Honey, tell me why you feel that way." His wife was stunned. It was the last thing she expected him to say. Did he really want to understand her? She decided to tell him. She explained that he was ignoring a lot of tasks around the house and leaving them all to her. She told him how overworked and underappreciated she felt. Mark just listened. His Voice of Fear wanted to defend him, but he knew that wouldn't create the results he wanted, so he just kept listening.

She said, "It's not fair, Mark. I have a full-time job, too, and I can't do everything. I need a little more help here." He told her that he understood why she felt that way. (He validated her.) She explained how unhappy and alone she felt. He asked what he could do to help out more. This shocked her, but she asked if he would be willing to take over two or three of the household tasks, and he agreed to. Then he asked her if she would be open to hearing how he felt about a couple of things (the permission question). She was cautious, but agreed because he was being so kind.

He told her that he had been feeling pretty alone, too. He told her that he wanted to work on their relationship and asked her if she would be willing to let past mistakes go and give each other a second chance. She agreed.

This was just the first of many conversations, and they occasionally still had a bad one, but they kept working on it. Mark recognized how powerful it was when he listened without getting defensive and making everything about him. This made his wife feel validated and important. He also learned the power of asking permission questions. His wife was much more open to hearing about his feelings when he asked permission first. Things did not change for them overnight, but within a few months they were significantly better. Mark shared with me the following quotes he found:

"The most important marriage skill is listening to your partner in a way that they can't possibly doubt that you love them."

—Dian Sollee

"Being heard is so close to being loved that for the average person, they are almost indistinguishable."

—David Augsburger

These are universal truths. When you show up in trust and give love by listening to your partner, they feel valued. When your partner feels valued, they are more capable of giving love back to you.

claritypoint: **If you want a good relationship, have mutually validating conversations on a daily basis.**

Love is a choice you must make about 500 times a day, though – whenever fear shows up in your head. If you can choose love in these moments instead of getting offended, hurt, or angry, your relationship will thrive; you will create a safe environment in which your partner can be imperfect and still be loved. You will also create this space for yourself.

claritypoint: **What counts most in your relationship is how you handle it when you offend each other. Handle these moments in trust and love, and you can work through anything.**

Choosing Clarity has taught you how to take responsibility for your behavior and your thinking. It has taught you to see yourself and your partner accurately and respond with trust, love, wisdom, and maturity. If you continue to read and reread this book, you will internalize the principles more and more and they will become a part of who you are.

Be sure to visit my website, www.claritypointcoaching. com, and download the *Choosing Clarity* worksheets. When you find yourself struggling with an offense or conflict, fill out the Clarity Questions Worksheet or the Forgiveness Formula before you do or say anything. It will help.

You might also want to create some new relationship rules. You might even want to get your partner involved and make these "relationship rules" policies together.

My Personal Policies about Relationships

This is my official policy about the role of my relationships in my life:

I am here to learn and love. The people in my life are here to teach me amazing lessons about love and help me become my best self. My partner is my greatest teacher. He is in a unique position to know me and help me become better. I do the same for him. My job is to see myself and my value accurately so I can be loving. My job is to see him, his value, and his behavior accurately and accept him as he is right now. I give him permission to be a work in progress, just like me. We are both students in the classroom of life and we both have a lot to learn.

This is my policy about my part in my relationship:

It is my responsibility to be the love in my relationship. I do not wait for my partner to step it up and apologize or show love — I do it first. It is my responsibility to value myself accurately and not make my self-esteem his job. I know my value is infinite and absolute and not on the line. I do not fear that he doesn't love me — I know he does even though in moments of fear he might not show it. My job is to make sure he feels loved and wanted every single day.

These are our official relationship rules:

1. I cannot change anyone else. In every moment I must work on fixing me, my thoughts, and my behavior. I must be more loving. That is the answer to every problem.

2. I step back from every situation and use the Clarity Formula to make sure I'm seeing myself, my partner, and the situation clearly and accurately. I do this before I do anything else.

3. When I feel hurt or offended, I use the Clarity Questions to help me find a love-based response.

4. I always use the Communication Formula when talking to my partner. We can have mutually validating conversations about anything. We can always find win/win solutions or compromises.

5. If we argue and feel like things are getting heated or we are going to a fear-based place, either of us can call a "time out." We both honor this and give the other person time to step back and get in Clarity before we continue the conversation.

6. Sometimes it's better to go to bed angry and wake up fresh than it is to talk about things in the moment. Clarity often comes with a good night's sleep.

7. When my partner mistreats me, I recognize that it is usually about their fear about their own value and is really a request for love or validation. I love my partner even when they don't deserve it.

8. I have already decided that the next time my partner offends me I will forgive them. I know that a good marriage is made of two good forgivers.

9. If I want more love, I give more love.

10. If I get angry at my partner, I fill out the You Spot It You Got It Worksheet. This helps me see my partner as the same as me.

11. I am committed to listening to my partner and validating their thoughts and feelings. Listening is the deepest way to show I value my partner.

12. I ask permission questions before I give my partner advice or tell them what I think.

13. I use more "I" statements than "you" statements, and I focus more on future behavior that is in my partner's control than past behavior that isn't.

The final step in the *Choosing Clarity* process is creating these new policies in your notebook and then making them part of your life by reviewing them and using them each day.

22 – Conclusion

*C*hoosing *Clarity* provided the opportunity to create powerful personal policies that can help you see and experience your life more clearly and accurately. Now I recommend that you review and reread your policies daily to keep them fresh in your mind. Set aside time every day to read through them, and after a while you won't need to read them anymore because you will know them by heart.

I also recommend that you don't stop reading this book just because you are at the end. It takes practice and repetition to internalize these universal principles into your subconscious thinking. You might even want to reread the book several times. My clients would tell you that repetition is the key to change. Each time you read *Choosing Clarity* you will pick up things you didn't get the first time.

In coaching, my clients receive amazing tools that further help them cement these principles into their subconscious thinking and change the emotions and habits that hold them back. You can experience some of that same transformation by reading your policies daily.

I also recommend that you practice using the Clarity Formula in every situation. Put your power to consciously choose your attitude to work, because the Voice of Fear in your head will continue to encourage fear-based thinking every day of your life. *Fear never takes a holiday. It never sleeps.* The good news is that the battle with fear gets easier the more you practice. Your ability to choose your mindset is like a muscle you have never used; right now it might even feel impossible to do. But I promise that if you keep working at choosing trust and love, it will get easier. The muscle will get in shape and you will be able to process your way to Clarity faster and faster. Just allow yourself to be a work in progress. You aren't meant to master it all right now. Just keep working at it and don't give up.

My greatest hope is that this book will make your life a little easier. I hope that through reading it you can now see clearly who you really are. I hope you have discovered your divine, amazing spirit side (your Voice of Truth), and have grasped what infinite and absolute value really means.

I hope you understand that love is literally the essence of your being. I hope that you feel inspired to set aside your fears and be more loving to the people in your life. In doing this you will discover who you really are.

I hope you trust life at a deeper level than ever before and that trust is giving you some strength and peace. I hope you have decided to experience life with a net. (It is a lot more fun that way!) I hope you can finally feel safe in the journey. I hope you understand that nothing can change your value; you are totally, completely perfect as you are right now.

I hope you can see life as a divine process to serve you, not as an evil force out to get you. I hope you can see that every experience is in your life for a reason – and that reason is to serve you. I hope you can go with the flow and trust the process of life more. When bad or scary things happen, choosing trust will make those tough times easier.

I hope you see the people and situations in your life more accurately and can see how fear drives their behavior. I hope you see them as the same as you. I hope you create less drama and conflict in your life because of this knowledge. I hope you resist applying your core fear where it doesn't belong, so you can choose trust and love instead of fear.

I really hope you share this book with everyone you know. I believe that learning the *Choosing Clarity* principles can make a difference in their lives. I hope that if enough of us share these principles with other people, it will create more peace on this earth. I believe principles of truth can do that. *They are the only thing that can.*

I also hope that you will write to me and tell me how *Choosing Clarity* has impacted your journey. You can write to me at kim@claritypointcoaching.com.

Please also visit my website where you will find articles about applying these principles to hundreds of specific situations. If you can't find the help you need, drop me a note.

Now I recommend that you start over and read *Choosing Clarity* again. The second time through you will pick up things you completely missed the first time.

As you reread the book, you can fine tune some of your policies (something you will want to do often). As you grow and learn, your policies will naturally evolve. You will also discover other areas of your life that deserve a new policy, so I have left you some room at the back of the book for other policies you want to create.

My team and I at Claritypoint Coaching are also available for personal and executive life coaching. The Claritypoint Coaching process takes what you have learned in *Choosing Clarity* to a much higher level and provides amazing tools for changing your subconscious programs.

You can contact us at www.claritypointcoaching.com for more information.

Endnotes

(Endnotes)

1 Frankl, *Man's Search for Meaning*, p. 86
2 *Man's Search for Meaning,* p. 135

49318821R00148

Made in the USA
San Bernardino, CA
20 May 2017